THE GREAT DEPRESSION

Mental Health

by Jacqueline Ivey

Dorrance Publishing Co
585 Alpha Drive
Suite 103
Pittsburgh, PA 15238
Visit our website at *www.dorrancebookstore.com*

ISBN: 979-8-8892-5345-7
eISBN: 979-8-8892-5845-2

THE GREAT DEPRESSION

Mental Health

Contents

Preface

I was persuaded that I was pretty well equipped to quench the fiery darts that might have been thrown at me. Of course, I hadn't anticipated, nor had I contemplated anyone's use of concrete objects, such as flaming darts that were implemented by the Romans, for they were made of hollow reeds with one end that had been cloaked and soaked in a flammable substance that was aimed and hurled to destroy the enemy. I knew very well that I had been conscientiously working to live a life that honors my God, Jehovah Rapha, my Healer and Restorer. So, why was I suffering? I hadn't realized that suffering is an integral part of the Christian life and that we suffer sometimes while doing "good" things.

Jesus even tells us in John 16:33, "I have said these things to you, that in me you may have peace. In the world you will have tribulation. But take heart; I have overcome the world." I now know that suffering has its purposes. Since we live in a fallen world and tend to be disobedient children at times, God treats us as the children we are. Just as an earthly father instructs his own to follow his rules, he reproves the child when the rule is violated. God's love is everlasting, and He uses a form of discipline to correct behaviors when necessary.

Perhaps we suffer because God wants us to draw nigh to Him or identify with others or be of encouragement. Experiencing suffering is necessary in preparing the Christian for ministry. In other words, we should make an effort to serve others as would Jesus. In 2 Corinthians 1:4, Paul says that God comforts us in all our affliction so that we may be able to comfort those who are in any affliction, with the comfort with which we ourselves are comforted by God.

Also, we suffer for the sake of our everlasting joy and His glory. God has His reasons for allowing things to happen. We may never know His reason or understand His wisdom, but we must trust His will.

Scriptures tell of many who were persecuted and suffered. To name a few, there were Job, Moses, Joseph, David and Paul, and many others suffered for His sake. Of course, I can never forget the One who suffered and paid the ultimate price for my sake! No matter what reasons we might think there are for suffering, we must know that earth is not our permanent home. God has a great plan for His elect.

Introduction

Long before I had known that the Bible says in Genesis that God created the male and the female in His own image, blessed and told them that they should be fruitful and multiply, I wanted a family of my own. My husband and I were married early in life. We eventually became loving parents to three handsome sons.

My dear husband, Mark, had earned a degree in Pharmacy in 1958 from Florida Agriculture and Mechanical University in Tallahassee, Florida, where we both had been students, and without delay he began to practice at a local pharmacy in Daytona Beach, Florida, a position that would last for ten years.

Unhappy with his 135-lb. frame, my husband consistently ate half-gallons of ice cream to gain weight. Little did he know, those pounds would pile on with age.

One day, after a long conversation with a friend who had become a practicing physician, my husband entered our home immediately and excitedly. He enthusiastically expressed a desire to become a medical doctor. I was not amused! Had we not just begun to purchase our first home six years earlier? What was I to do with three young sons while he was away in Nashville, Tennessee? We had never been apart! How was I to run the household alone? I had never seen a bill, let alone paid one. I knew the cost of nothing. I had never even opened the mailbox. Who would mow the lawn, put gas into my car and wash and wax it? So many questions filled and swirled around in my head. Surely, I could not be supportive of such an idea! I loved my husband fervently, and we must not be separated by the hundreds of miles. Nonetheless, I reluctantly agreed to stay behind with our sons, who were eleven, eight and two years old. Had I a choice? No, not really, since I was the only adult with no means of income but my teacher's salary.

After four additional years of medical education and four more years of internship and residency in obstetrics and gynecology in Akron, Ohio, we returned to the Sunshine State, settled in, and we both resumed our livelihoods in 1978 in Lakeland, Florida. Mark began his medical practice while I taught at a middle high school, which was a hop and skip from our home.

The Great Depression
Introduction

I had not come to grips with the purpose of my suffering for years. I truly had not looked upon it analytically. But through the years of learning about God's purposes and having a closer communion with Him, I believe I better understand as I look retrospectively over the years of my life. Could I have been devoting more attention to the gift than to the Word of God? If so, I would have been committing an atrocious offense. I have learned that this behavior strips God of His holiness. He is the Creator of all things and all things belong to Him! He is not merely a god, He is the one and only God! I cannot recall any time that God had not been superior to anyone or anything. I knew that I never wanted to walk this earth without God in my life. I cannot recall not offering my supplications up to Him. In our home, at an early age my mother had taught me to pray. When my late husband and I were married, I loved him dearly and cared for him lovingly. I was and am convinced that he was God's gift to me, plucked from His flock. We find in James 1:17 that every good and perfect gift comes from the Father. I could not have imagined life without him. Nonetheless, I found him slipping away from my arms of everlasting love.

Mark was not a perfect man, but he was perfect for me. When we were united as one, he took the helm of the Ivey household and led extremely well. His love was sincere. He was a believer who greatly loved his family. He was handsome, talented, a toiler, quick-witted, an intellectual marvel, a true provider, caregiver, and was full of frivolity and humor, but to his detriment he was often dilatory when attending events. At times when he, our children and I were approaching the stop sign at the entrance of our subdivision and were compelled to wait for passage of a number of vehicles before it was safe to exit, many times he'd say, "Now, they could have passed by here when I was in the shower." The drivers would become the scapegoats if we were late for an event. Of course, it all was his tongue-in-cheek humor.

As the father of our sons, he was unlike his austere father, but very much like his imperturbable mother, who was slow to anger, but quick to reclaim his serenity if he had become agitated. My husband's father was a Christian and a citrus foreman at a local packing company. He was the disciplinarian of his household. He inculcated in his sons the importance of working hard, moral and intellectual skills. He also served as PTA president of his three young sons' school and remained in that capacity for thirty-six years. My husband's mild-mannered, deeply Christian and ultraconservative mother, who was employed by the Marion County, Florida, School Board, taught him about Christianity, and in the little white-frame one-room public schoolhouse, she taught him academics during his early years among other students in the nearby township of Summerfield, Florida. The mixed ages and abilities classes allowed students to more quickly grasp basic skills and knowledge at all levels in this environment. At an early age, Mark graduated from Howard Academy in Ocala. His formative years were spent in a vast, essentially pastural community, which backdropped and influenced his development. My wonderful husband and our sons' hands-on father was someone we will always remember lovingly. After spending a few weeks at Florida State University upon his high school graduation, our youngest son had expressed many times that he had more fun with his parents than at the university, and our sons were first to recognize that their father's parenting style very much resembled that of the main character and head of the family on *The Cosby Show*, Dr. Heathcliff "Cliff" Huxtable. Dr. Mark Ivey III was easy to love, is impossible to forget and irreplaceable!

Chapter 1
My Husband, Mark, Leaves for Medical School

It was 1969 when my husband, Mark Ivey III, was accepted as a student into the School of Medicine at Meharry Medical College in Nashville, Tennessee. He had applied late. As a result, his receipt of a letter of acceptance was in the late summer of 1969. His notice of resignation and preparation to leave his position as a pharmacist for the past ten years was nearly effortless. On the other hand, I instantly knew that my role as manager of the household and the lone parent of our three young sons would be challenging.

We had learned that one of our young neighbors, who lived merely two doors away, would be returning to Tennessee State University to continue his education. So Mark and our very gentlemanly soft-spoken neighbor agreed to share an apartment for Mark's first year. I yet had to apply for and obtain a teaching position. Once I had secured employment, our sons and I would join him.

We both knew that his needs would be many to begin this journey, so I shopped frugally for Mark's numerous needs for his new living conditions and for attire that would be appropriate for weather that would be in contrast to the subtropical climate of the central parts of Florida and "The Volunteer State," which could be considerably colder with moderate snowfalls during the winter months.

Sometime earlier, Mark and another former graduate of Howard Academy in Ocala, Florida, had learned of each other's plan to enter this historically second-largest educator of African-American medical doctors and dentists in the United States. I was to drive my husband to Ocala, near his birthplace, for this rendezvous with his friends, Lemuel and Runette, and the three of them would make the trip to Nashville, Tennessee.

Finally, the day arrived for my husband's departure. At the first flush of morning, I rose to prepare breakfast for our family of five and lunch for Mark's approximate 637-mile drive to Nashville. Suddenly, the imminence of his embarkation became a painful reality. As I stood in our kitchen assembling his lunch, I became weak at the knees and felt nauseous and began to vomit consistently. It was apparent that the symptoms were definitely emotional and physical issues, and now, even more so, because I was thoroughly incapable of making the jaunt to Ocala and would not set eyes upon my husband again before Christmas. Nonetheless, an immediate phone call to my dear mother, Madge Butler, who lived only three blocks away, brought her to my side. When she had served my family breakfast and packed Mark's lunch, she drove Mark to Ocala, and our children would have the privilege of seeing him off. As I remained at home, I cried out wildly in disappointment!

Later, during that day, I made an urgent telephone call to my mother-in-law's home. I simply had to hear Mark's voice once again before their long drive. Unfortunately he, Lemuel and Runette had begun that laborious drive. I began to sob uncontrollably. My mother-in-law, Mazie, sincerely lamented, "I don't see why Mark couldn't take you all with him," but she knew that I solely had to support our family since my husband's days soon would be occupied with a very demanding schedule.

The first week passed and my employment as an educator made weekdays more palatable during Mark's absence. However, weekends were almost intolerable. I wept ceaselessly. The Saturday of the first weekend that Mark left, I lay in bed and sobbed bitterly. I vividly recall that our eight-year-old son entered my bedroom and naively asked, "Mommy, why are you cryin'?" Before I could respond, forthwith our eleven-year-old followed him into the bedroom to assuage his fears and opined, while gently taking him by the hand, "Mommy has a headache," as he led Marlon away. Although I became a believer at thirteen years of age, I knew very little Scripture, and that, which I had learned, was simply memorized. I had not known how to apply the Word, be strong in the Lord and in His mighty power (Ephesians 6:10), nor did I know that I can do all things through Christ Jesus who strengthens me (Philippians 4:13). I had sung the words "I am weak but He is strong. Yes, Jesus loves me" regularly as a tiny tot but had not comprehended its meaning fully to incorporate it into my faith. Had I the knowledge of God's promises, I would have found comfort and strength in Him.

On Sundays, we would frequently attend morning church services with Mother, and during the evenings she would visit probably for an hour before leaving and returning to her home. Since my extremely modest salary allowed us to barely muddle through, I unfortunately took some Lord Days to prepare for some weeks that followed for lawn care, lesson plans, bulletin boards and other pertinent activities that would not permit me to perform during the other six days of the week, although I had been taught that six days shall thy labor and rest on the Sabbath.

Later, the boys, in their pajamas, would gather in front of the television to watch their favorite program that they had often viewed with their father, Mutual of Omaha's Wild Kingdom. Marlin Perkins, an American zoologist, was best known as a host of the television program. I, too, watched while waiting anxiously for my husband's seven-o' clock visit by telephone. He and I often spoke for roughly two hours, reviewing the past events of the week and declaring our passionate love for each another every Lord's Day.

Then, there was the summer of 1969, when I sat and watched the news alone while our three sons slept. This was news that captured the world that no one would soon forget. I listened conscientiously as the anchor reported on the horrific deaths of Sharon Tate and others that were conducted by cult leader Charles Manson. Tate was a young, novel actress and model, who was most famous for her role in *Valley of the Dolls*. She also was married to filmmaker Roman Polanski and nearly nine months pregnant. Friends had been invited to stay with Tate while Polanski was away on business. During this time, Manson ordered Charles "Tex" Watson to go to the mansion with others and murder its occupants. I don't truly know why, nor do I remember the true motive the villains might have had, except for the pleasure of slaughtering. Nonetheless, Manson had ordered his subservient followers, or family, to kill them all. When they had brutally shot and stabbed Tate and her friends, one took blood from the victim and wrote "PIG" on the front door. This was their passion, part of their religion and plans to travel around America and kill families in their homes. I had been petrified with fear.

Some months later, Jeffrey R. MacDonald, an Army Special Forces physician, claimed three males and a female walked through an unlocked door to his Fort Bragg, North Carolina, apartment. He asserted the scoundrels attacked him, his wife and two- and five-year-old daughters with clubs, ice picks and knives. Each family member had been stabbed multiple times, bludgeoned, and the wounds were of such severe nature that they died immediately after infliction. When the massacre was over, the culprits allegedly took MacDonald's deceased wife's blood to write "PIG" on the headboard of the couple's bed. Some wondered if this were a created copycat story of the Manson murders. Nevertheless, again I was gripped by fear by the account of the gore and slaughter of this pregnant mother and her young girls that I telephoned my mother, who lived on the same street only three blocks away. "Mother, please come spend the night with the boys and me," I implored. "No, you have got to learn to live on your own," as she began to gently reprove my lack of faith and fear. I had no other option except to sleep at home, in my bed alone, with my sons in the bedroom down the hallway.

After a restless night of cowering in bed, I awoke early morning, took a hot bath, prepared breakfast and dressed the boys for school. Michael, our two-year-old, was accustomed to spending the day with my mother. I also dropped off the two older boys and they walked to school, which was approximately two blocks from Mother's home, and I continued to school. I hadn't felt too well as the day grew late. I surmised I had entered the cold, wintry air too soon after a hot bath that morning since this was uncustomary. I had begun to feel ill with a scratchy throat and body pain. I could not ascertain if it were influenza, sinusitis or a very bad cold, but I knew for certain I was downright miserable. Consequently, once again I telephoned Mother and, of course, she had too much compassion to leave me and her grands to fend for ourselves alone; so she graciously was willing to assume my responsibilities at my home, caring for us all. Clearly, excessive fear can affect one's physical and emotional health as was mine. I know now that there are many Scriptures in God's Word that encourage and give us hope when we are in need. "God is our refuge and strength and an ever-present help in trouble" (Psalm 56:1). We must know that for all there will be difficult experiences and challenges and times that will test and shape our faith, but know that we can grow from our suffering, which is what God wants for His children.

Mark returned for Christmas after four months of academic drudgery. We all embraced his homecoming with flaming exhilaration! Of course, he was most appreciative and proud of my leadership without him. All of the bills were consistently paid in a timely manner. The end of the driveway that puddled had been repaired. Our sons and I had meticulously manicured the lawn. Even our two-year-old, Michael, had assisted with the clearing away of pinecones. The lawn was a plush green carpet. I had done some painting, the house was spotless, the colorful Christmas tree sat in front of the huge picture window with perfectly wrapped gifts nestled below. Much of this achievement was exemplary because my thoughtful husband had left a little black tablet on the kitchen stove to advise and remind me of my responsibilities that were virtually new to me.

After the celebratory season, it was time for each of us to return to the joys of real life.

On my husband's return to Nashville, he was compelled to drive his 1963 black-and-white Jaguar XKE Convertible. He needed his personal transportation to move from one place to another while in the Music City. My stomach seemed comforted, but I could not erase the horrible visual that this very low vehicle could be sandwiched and crushed between semi-trucks. That's an 18-wheeler, and I had envisioned that my husband's inability to navigate the very low coupe over the slick roads during winter could be fatal! I was convinced that he could easily lose control and sent barreling down the snow-covered mountainside. He was a Floridian! He was a resident of the Sunbelt and had no experience maneuvering through snow-covered roads, hills or mountains. I was driven with the fear of losing the love of my life! Nonetheless, I waited for the ring of the phone to hear, "I am here!" I had not yet known that "God gave us a spirit not of fear but of power and love and self-control" (1 John 4:18 ESV). While I saw us as Christians, no promises and few verses of Scripture did I know or understand.

It was then the summer of 1970. Mark had one year of medical school that he had completed and had done extremely well. So he came home to Daytona Beach, Florida, to retrieve his family. I had made arrangements for our fairly new home to be rented since we would have liked to return to our comfortable abode, following Mark's acquisition of his medical degree and specialty in obstetrics and gynecology. He could possibly begin his medical practice in Daytona Beach.

Finally, school was over for summer, and the vision of our togetherness again thrilled me, but there was much to be done. We sold some furniture, gave some to my mother-in-law and my mother for safekeeping. Mark and I carefully packed boxes of remaining items, and he loaded the rented U-Haul while I meticulously cleaned the house. Oh, oh, the chickens! Mother had gifted Mark IV and Marlon with baby chicks for Easter, and we could not leave those behind since the boys loved them so much. The biddies had really grown and habitually followed our two older sons to the neighborhood store and home again or wherever they might have wandered. The domesticated Gallus had known no others of their genus. Since there was no way to shelter these now hens, I hired a carpenter to construct a coop for the two adult female chickens to provide a safe space for them to live safely, away from predators.

We had planned to spend the night at Mother's house the night before leaving so that ours would be immaculate for our renters. Surprisingly, my buoyant, stalwart mother did something I had never witnessed before, nor could I have ever fathomed in my wildest dreams. Powerless to accept her only daughter and her family's abandonment of home and city, my mother fled by boarding an airplane to Wisconsin to escape the agony of seeing our departure. I had seen my beautiful mother, one of great faith, funeralize her father, mother, husband and two brothers with optimum strength and courage. Now I wondered if her children could have been my indomitable mother's proverbial Achilles' heel. It is a surety that our faith is tested on the things of this world and the rest.

The following day, we rose fairly early in the morning to begin our migration to Nashville.

The boys chose to ride in the big truck with their dad and decided that the chickens would be safer with me. Certainly, the chickens could not ride in the rear of the truck with no ventilation.

We drove until the setting sun was bathed in hues of red and orange and began to sink behind tall buildings and trees. We carefully sought and found a local motel to spend the night.

The following morning, we readied ourselves for the continuation of our journey. We walked out into the parking lot. I unlocked the doors to my beige sedan Chevrolet and swung open the passenger's side to put in and secure my now-three-year-old. We didn't see the chickens that were left to spend the night there. My mouth was agape and my eyes widened. Our sons were truly in a state of disbelief. One of the older sons opened the back door, leaned forward and peeked inside. Wow, what a stench! There were droppings almost everywhere. We laughed nervously in repugnance, but they only had done what comes naturally. Nonetheless, the chickens had hidden beneath the front seats of the vehicle to escape the torrid mid-morning sun. Thank God they were safe, and we did not have to hear the cries of our young sons, which could have been for an additional three hundred miles. In our effort to create a trip that suggested comfort and leisure for our family, we had forgotten about the children's pets.

Chapter 2
All Together Again in the Music City

Finally, we arrived in Nashville, the capital city, Music City, the home of the Grand Ole Opry House, Opryland, Fisk University, Meharry Medical School, Vanderbilt, Tennessee State University, Belmont University and others. Nashville had been given the name "Athens of the South" because of its focus on education. This would be the place we would call home for the next few years.

Once we were there, we carefully unpacked our belongings and began to settle into the rather hilly Cumberland Gardens area. The 1951 brick structure, where we would reside was a mere 875-square-foot, three-bedroom, one-bath, single-family dwelling. We were just minutes away from the Cumberland River that snaked and flowed west below the Clarksville Pike, thus the name of the subdivision "Cumberland Gardens."

Following Mark's admission to Meharry, I applied for a teaching position, and when I visited my husband during the spring break I was interviewed. An approximate two weeks later, I had learned that I had been employed by the Davidson County School Board; however, the National Teacher Exam (NTE) was in effect, and I yet had to be subjected to and pass that examination since the NTE was a requirement and part of the teacher licensing process. I thank God that I successfully passed the somewhat rigid test and was assigned to

Gra-Mar Elementary School, which was about eight to nine miles away from our home in Cumberland Gardens.

I enrolled all of our sons in their respective schools. They seemed to enjoy the school days at first. However, one evening, while we all sat at our dining table to eat together as a family, our oldest son sat quietly, fumbled with his fork, twirled it in his food and move it aimlessly around on his plate. I probed, "Mark, why aren't you eating? What's wrong?"

"I can't. It hurts to eat," he softly replied.

"What happened?"

"A boy at school hit me there," he said hesitantly.

"Why?" I asked angrily.

He further explained that this child had taken his seat when he had walked away, but the seventh-grade instructor advised the young boy to return to his assigned seat. He was furious, and after school the ill-tempered bully maliciously attacked my son, who and been taught to report such incidents to the one who's in authority. I was irate!

The following morning, I contacted the principal at the school where I taught to inform the principal that I had an urgent matter that I must address, but I would report to school immediately after the parent-principal conference.

I flounced into the principal's office at Wharton Junior School and introduced myself. With careful detail, I laid out the events that had taken place in one of my son's classrooms the day before and the aftermath. His welcoming demeanor shifted to intimidation. He seemed daunted to take action against the troubled youth. He explained why Parent-Teacher Association meetings were held during the day rather than evening. Reportedly, there had been acts of violence, and youth had vandalized vehicles during the night. Angrily I said, "If you are afraid to do anything about this occurrence, I will call the police!" "Let me call his mother and talk with her, Mrs. Ivey," he eagerly suggested.

That evening, I received a telephone call from the adolescent's mother, who earnestly begged, "Please don't call the police. It won't happen again." Profoundly touched by her sincerity, I relented and said that it must *never* happen again.

I had counted it all a blessing that we would reside in Cumberland Gardens. Our home was at the corner of Twenty-sixth Avenue and Salem Mason Drive. We were simply steps away from the neighborhood school, John Early Elementary. When our youngest was old enough, he and his older brother would simply cross the street, walk through the gate and they're there in a jiffy. On the southeast side of the school grounds was the recreation area.

Earlier in the day during that summer, our oldest son sought permission to play on the court at John Early Elementary School, that school that was merely a stone's throw away from our home, across the street. My response was an emphatic "No!" He ignored my "no" to his request. The passing of time was short before I heard the kitchen door fling open. "Mom, Mom!" he cried while stumbling into the house and cupping his hand over his bleeding left eye. A youth in the neighborhood and he had been playing together. When Mark decided to return to his home, the young boy called out to him, "Hey, Mark!" Mark turned toward him in response. The naive child had clasped a rather small piece of corrugated fiberboard in his hand that he carefully aimed and sent it sailing through the air before cutting into my son's eye. I was devastated and furious! It is easy to determine that I was an alarmist. Unlike David, the psalmist, I had not learned to turn to the Lord in times of trouble, knowing that He is my strength. I had not realized that He is my deliverer and stronghold. What knowledge I lacked of God's holy Word!

So I took Mark to an ophthalmologist at Meharry immediately. After a thorough examination and inspection of the retina, macula and optic nerve, speaking in a most normal voice that he could muster and with effort to not alarm me further, he advised, "The vision in his left eye is 20/500, and there's bleeding behind the retina." How could I accept the possibility of my twelve-year-old having only one eye?!!! His whole life was ahead of him. I could not comfort nor calm my fears that the youth's reckless act would result in my son's blindness in his eye.

When we returned home from the doctor's office, I telephoned my praying mother and mother-in-law. Both showed so much compassion and expressions of sorrow and regret. Each of these two faithful servants of God shared this unfortunate circumstance with their Christian friends. I had heard both of them pray innumerably, and they both were of the persuasion that God could do anything except fail. I had heard my mother-in-law pray again and again Psalm 37:4, "Delight yourself in the Lord and He shall give you the desires of your heart," but many years would pass before I really grasped the true meaning of that Scripture, but Mazie Ivey, my mother-in-law, had known for many years since she had taught Bible studies. Not until I attended our church shepherding group had I learned its meaning. This group had begun and continually meets on the second Lord's Day of each month as it did years ago when Elder Michael Akin asked the small flock the meaning of that verse. It was clearly said that to delight one's self in the Lord means that we are to take our minds off our own circumstances and desires and long for the those things that He wants. Then, He will give you the desires of your heart. He wants us to want more of Him. I think Matthew 6:33 really puts it in perspective: "We are to seek first the kingdom of God and His righteousness, and all these things will be added to you." I must not focus on the latter of part Psalm 37:4, but the first. God wants us to want more of Him first. It is apparent that these two prayer warriors had known this, and they and their friends prayed fervently, and so did I. I truly had learned the power of faith and supplication. By the way, succinctly the shepherding groups are small groups that are ministered to and prayed for by its elder. Small groups also permit members to grow in friendship more personally, and according to the Constitution of the Presbyterian Church, elders are instructed to engage members in the mission of the church and to provide opportunities for evangelism, pastoral care, worship, education and stewardship.

For our next appointed time, we returned to the ophthalmologist's office for a follow-up examination. The doctor turned to me and announced extremely joyfully that my son's vision was now 20/50. With kindness and measureless gratitude, I fell upon him and thanked him profusely. Denying all credit for this miracle, "Mrs. Ivey, I had nothing to do with it!" he declared. I knew it had to have been the prayers of the saints.

Although I had left Turie T. Small Elementary in Daytona Beach, Volusia County, Florida, where the struggle to desegregate had just taken place a year earlier, I found that I was once again facing a similar situation. It had been in May of 1954 that the U.S. Supreme Court ruled racial segregation in schools to be unconstitutional in its landmark Brown v. Board of Education ruling. To end segregation had been the Supreme Court's unanimous decision. Three years later, in 1957, the public schools of Nashville, Tennessee, began to end segregation when they executed a "stairstep" plan that began with a choice representation of first-graders, and a grade was added until all of the twelve grades were desegregated. Many of my colleagues with whom I talked were livid that segregation would be ending. Could it have been the thought of the intermingling of the races and possible dwindling of a white society? Could some have believed that it could have been the end of white supremacy or superiority over the black race, or was there fear of criminal behavior or a conglomerate of all of the above? As for me, I was sincerely ecstatic. I could only marvel at the idea of teachers and students no longer being separate and unequal among other reasons. Nonetheless, I recall at least a bomb scare at one of my schools. All were forced to evacuate the buildings and assemble orderly on the school ground. That was utterly terrifying! Notwithstanding, the rest of that year and the years that followed were exemplary.

Chapter 3
Revelation of Mother's Cancer and Symptoms of Obvious Anxiety

Mark had nearly completed his four years of medical school. He decided that he would either choose pathology or obstetrics and gynecology as his specialty. Geography was as crucial as the "right" hospital. Practically all of one summer we had searched across three states to select a hospital that offered one of the very best programs for internship and the three-year commitment in obstetrics and gynecology. Since we both would be working parents to three young sons, it was paramount that the schools were within walking distance of our home. Another aspect to consider was the issue of safety. From personal observation, it appeared that smaller cities tend to be safer places with lower crime rates than larger or more populous cities. So when Mark graduated with his Doctor of Medicine degree, we left Nashville, arrived and settled in Akron, Ohio, the "rubber capital of the world."

On June 1, 1973, Mark began his training at Akron General Medical Center (AGMC). I applied for a teaching position with Summit County Public Schools and was hired immediately. At the end of that summer, I registered and enrolled our sons, Michael, Marlon and Mark IV, in Erie Island Elementary, Perkins Junior High and Buchtel High Schools respectively as new students.

As was customary, my precious mother came to visit us during the Christmas holidays and again at the end of the school year. We all were sitting in the living room when she complained that she had a dull pain in the bottom of her stomach. She compared this discomfort to menstrual cramps that she had experienced from years gone by. My husband and I, as well as she, knew that at the age of sixty-nine years she was menopausal. My husband, now a doctor of medicine, suggested with strong uneasiness, "Madge, why won't you let me examine you?" Mother replied with slight indignation, "Huh, you must be crazy. I'm not going to let you examine me!" He said to her then, "If you won't let me examine you, make sure your gynecologist does as soon as you return to Daytona." She gave him her word that she would.

It was late afternoon when I had returned home from a day's work at school. It, too, was my birthday and several days after Mother's return to her home in Florida. After parking my car near our detached garage, I sauntered up to the house and thrust open the storm door to the kitchen. I stepped in front of it, stopping it as it struck against my back. Then, I unlocked the kitchen door. Startled, I asked my husband, "What are you doing here?" for it was far too early to see him at home. He did not attempt to candy-coat his response, "Madge has endometrial carcinoma!" he blurted out. "Oh, no!" I began to wail bitterly. I had never known my mother to have any ailment that was greater than a headache. I was persuaded that this cancer of the uterus was a death sentence. If you have ever heard of Alexander Pope's idiomatic expression "A little learning is a dangerous thing," this is a definite truism. Since I was the wife of a physician, I had gained merely enough knowledge about some medicine that I might behave in a manner that could be to my own detriment. I had no sisters or brothers. I had grown up with a stepfather, but this was my biological mother, my confidante. She had doted upon me all of my life and showered me with much affection, hugs and kisses. She had prayed with and for me innumerably, and all that I knew she had taught me.

Life would never be the same without her! I had recalled saying that I wanted to be buried with her if anything were to happen to her. I wish I had known then that God has not given us a spirit of fear. Nonetheless, my extremely wise mother was well aware of my predisposition to fear or worry excessively. So when Dr. Cochran, an outstanding caregiver and gynecologist, had made the accurate diagnosis, Mother asked him to contact her son-in-law at Akron Regional Medical Center so that he could reveal the news to her daughter, and of course, that kind of dreadfully devastating information should *not* have been shared over the telephone. That was the reason that my loving husband arrived at home so early on my birthday. I had not been able to ascertain if I were having anxiety or panic attacks, but I do know that each time that I became intensely fearful the effects were physical. I either had become nauseous, experienced palpitations, fluttery of the stomach, insomnia, loss of appetite and/or headaches.

Our oldest son had purchased all of the fixings to make my birthday an extraordinary one, but I had no appetite, nor had I a reason to celebrate—not now. A dark cloud had enveloped my entire being. My heart had begun to palpitate, butterflies were in my stomach, and my head had begun to ache. After my husband Mark and my brief exchange, I placed my purse and other items away before taking a seat in everyone's favorite velvet upholstered rocking chair in the living room. I sat quietly and cried ceaselessly. I consumed no food for three days except for the very few treats our son, Mark, insisted I eat from the would-be party. I deeply regretted not being in a state of mind to commemorate the day of my birth, especially since our teenage son had planned and diligently hosted the big surprise so jubilantly and beautifully. There were no worries about the leftovers. Having three sons at home, all of the party food magically disappeared.

Some few weeks later, Mother was scheduled for a hysterectomy. We were told that the cancerous area was well differentiated. This meant that the cancer cells resembled the normal cells from which they grew, and this would be a better prognosis than undifferentiated cancers. Dr. Cochran, the gynecologist, said that the cancerous growth was about the size of a quarter. He removed the uterus surgically. Mother's recovery was approximately six weeks. I was eternally thankful and relieved. God is forever gracious and merciful! My anxiety was lifted.

Since the surgical procedure had taken place just prior to the beginning of another school year, our three sons and I traveled by Amtrak to DeLand, Florida, and were picked up by our sons' godfather and taken to Daytona, which was approximately twenty-three miles between the two small cities. I took care of my mother for the week that I was there before returning to Akron for the new school year. I left our oldest son, Mark IV, in Daytona Beach. He was prepared to enter Florida Agriculture and Mechanical University (FAMU) in Tallahassee, Florida. However, this would be his first year since he had just recently graduated from Buchtel High School in Akron, and FAMU classes would not commence for several more weeks.

Chapter 4
Ripped Apart Once Again

Mark and I were poised for the last year of his internship and residency. He was excited that he would soon begin his medical practice, and I could hardly wait to leave the Snow Belt and return to the Sun Belt, a region of a sunny and a somewhat tropical climate, where gardening is possible throughout the year. I had found such delight in seeing beautiful colorful vegetation. Sable palms stood majestically along the sandy coastline of Florida. Their very large leaves that varied from a bright to deep olive green grew right from the trunk, spreading in all directions as they sheltered beachgoers from the piercing-hot rays of the sultry sun. Magnificent flowering trees and brilliant colors of flowers that represented every color of the rainbow dotted the Florida landscape and green manicured lawns with infinite beauty. I yearned to return to that, the splendor I had not noticed before. For many days out of a year in Akron, there was no visible sun. During those days, I was more emotional and somewhat depressed, especially after holidays and when it was time to return to work. Those episodes of melancholy were more prevalent right after the Christmas Season and New Year's Day. During menstrual cycles, I wanted my beloved to just hold me lovingly in his arms, or I would begin to well up and the tears would flow uncontrollably.

At any rate, our hopes were dashed and our spirits were crushed when the Chairman of the Department of Obstetrics and Gynecology at Akron General Medical Center (AGMC) informed my husband that he would not renew his contract for another year, which was to be Mark's final year of residency. When I received the ruinous news, I threw my hands up. "What!? Why? What do we do now!?" I don't recall that my husband ever gave me a reason for his dismissal, but unlike me he seemed unruffled, but that was his way, skillful in concealing his true feelings. Between the two of us, he was always the stalwart and resilient one, at least he appeared to be.

How he so quickly became a physician at the Mound Bayou Community Hospital in the extremely small community of Mound Bayou, Mississippi, a self-sufficient African-American town of an only estimated 1,000 residents, I wouldn't have envisioned! On the other hand, he had spent six weeks earlier as a student, when Meharry had sent its students there for a learning experience.

Once again, our sons and I would be alone. This time, we were in a big city with a population of approximately 300,000 with no other relatives. Of course, Nashville was a big city, too. Nevertheless, we all had made wonderful friends. Soon, it was time for Mark's departure to Mound Bayou. I cried daily before he was to leave. I was extremely heartbroken. My effort to concentrate was fruitless. I had found no pleasure in the teaching that I had openly boasted for the years I had taught in the Akron Public Schools. My joy had fully faded and withered. Too quickly and too soon it was Sunday, the day Mark was to drive to Mound Bayou, Mississippi, in his three-year-old Jaguar, the V-12 E-type Roadster, the automobile he'd gifted himself for graduation from medical school. As before, I worried that some monstrous truck would not see him, or he'd be forced off the road and tumble down the mountainside, and I could get that dreadful call of his death. This was an image that I could not erase. As we both sat at the foot of our bed, he tried to muster the courage to leave. Mark tried frenziedly to find humor in it all to brighten my mood as he watched the Rolaids television commercial that many would recall, "How does America spell relief?"

"For heartburn? We spell it R-o-l-a-i-d-s!"

Mark turned to me and asked, "Hey, Jack, how does America spell relief?" Through my tears, "For heartache? M-a-r-k!" He smiled enormously.

He sat with me far beyond his scheduled parting, trying to comfort me. I relented because there was no need to put off the inevitable any longer.

He left and I was miserable. Day after day, I began to feel some discomfort in my chest. My heart would not stop racing, and the flutters in my stomach were forever present. I knew that I needed to see a physician. I made the earliest appointment that was available prior to the beginning of my school day. I was examined and diagnosed with anxiety. You see, sometimes fear can be so irrational and unfounded that it interferes with one's ability to live normally. Although I had grown up in the Church, I did not know that when I am afraid I put my trust in Him (Psalm 56:3 ESV). Anyway, my doctor prescribed Elavil, a medicine used to treat symptoms of depression. I was instructed to take one at bedtime to sleep. It was apparent that the dosage was too strong when the effects had not worn off at the end of the following school day and I was still drowsy and stumbling.

When I returned to my physician, he was made aware of the negative effects of Elavil. He advised me to discontinue the taking of this drug and prescribed a low dosage of Valium, another medication that is designed to treat anxiety and anxiety-related issues. This medicine, too, induces sedation and helps one fall asleep.

I telephoned my husband, who was now in Mound Bayou earning a salary to assist in supporting his family. He suggested that I wait until the weekend to take a broken-in-half tablet and observe my reaction on that Saturday morning. When I overslept on Saturday until about noon, that was evidence that even one half the dosage proved to be too potent. I refused to take any more and dealt as best as I could with the persistent symptoms. Blessedly, the impact of my husband's leaving suddenly subsided over time.

My lack of appetite and poor eating habits sometimes contributed to my illness, and we all were unfamiliar with the colder and drier weather in the Buckeye State. I contracted influenza. Nonetheless, I had three sons who were depending on me. With a sore throat, chills and fever and too weak to stand, I dragged a chair up to the kitchen stove to sit while preparing dinner, and between carefully turning meats and scarcely stirring the pots I gingerly laid my head on the back of the chair.

When the Summit County folk dance instructor for teachers in the elementary schools learned of my illness, she bulldozed her way through the inches of freshly fallen snow to our home with a full meal for my family and me. Food that was ready to eat for more than just that one night were the delectable chicken soup, dessert and the beverage. My three sons ate voraciously. I recovered and regained enough strength to return to school in time and dance again with the teachers' dance group that performed in the city's various venues. Eventually I was my old self again.

We were nearing Christmastime again in 1975, and I'd just followed through with my responsibility to sponsor the Christmas programs at Barber and Fraunfelter Elementary Schools, where I taught. For many weeks, the students and I had worked painstakingly to achieve an impeccable performance. Classroom time was used for instruction of songs, even four-part harmony, and we arrived at school an hour prior to the scheduled school time for rehearsals. Also, I'd spent weekends creating all of the costumes. Our Barber Elementary School art instructor constructed the backdrop, and finally it was "showtime"! The programs were successes! I was told by many of my colleagues that I made it look so easy or that there hadn't been a program, but a production! Of course, I was flattered, but tired, and yearly I wound up with laryngitis from the constant singing and teaching.

Now that the first school semester was in the rear, the real hustle and bustle had begun. I had to prepare for Mark's and Mother's arrivals from Daytona Beach, Florida, and Mound Bayou, Mississippi, respectively. There were shopping to be done, housecleaning, decorating of the Christmas tree and cooking for the time we believers celebrate the birth of Christ.

The boys and I met Mother at the Akron Bus Station on the day of her arrival, and on the day that my husband and our children's father's airliner was to land. We piled into the car, and I drove thirty miles north of Akron, Ohio, to the Cleveland Hopkins International Airport to meet with him. Needless to say, our meeting together again was utter excitement and enjoyment.

During the eve of Christmas, I could be found desperately trying to quietly wrap gifts without disturbing our sons' sleep, which continued until early morning on Christmas Day. It seemed as though I'd only finished the wrapping of presents before the boys were viciously tearing the wrappings away. On the other hand, some items were too large to be enveloped.

Christmas Day was filled with thanksgiving, joy and laughter. Dinner was served, and the traditional golden-brown roasted turkey was the centerpiece of the dining table. Other fitting essentials were cornbread dressing, pilaf rice, collard greens, sweet potato souffle, macaroni and cheese, cranberry sauce, iced tea, and we topped the meal off with the Southern sweet potato pie.

Unfortunately, when my mother and husband left after what appeared to be a very short visit with us at Christmastime, I cried and cried, feeling nothing except gloom, and a deeper depression set in once again.

One weekend as I sat in front of the television at home, I received a much unexpected telephone call. I was astounded! The Chairman of the Department of Obstetrics and Gynecology at Akron Regional Medical Center was calling. He asked about Mark, his whereabouts and his contact number. I happily provided this information and excitedly hurried to telephone him before the Department Chair could, but I was already too late. I received a busy tone. So I waited eagerly for Mark's call since the Chairman of the Department of Obstetrics and Gynecology had not divulged the nature of his call. Sure enough, when their conversation ended my telephone rang. Mark gladly shared that he had been invited to return to AGMC. This meant he would complete his residency where it had begun almost three years earlier, and we all would be under the same roof once more. We all were overjoyed, thankful and blessed! I never knew the reason for Mark's dismissal in the first place. Now that I think of it, his greatest character flaw was procrastination. Could it have been his invariable tardiness?!!

Chapter 5
Mark's Injury when He Erroneously Lifted a Lawnmower

The following year, when Mark had completed his final year of residency, we relocated to Lakeland, Florida, arriving on a Saturday. On Monday, my husband began his new position, Dr. Mark Ivey, Obstetrics and Gynecology, having joined the team of Drs. John S. Jackson and W. O. Blake. However, this piece of architecture had not been designed to accommodate three physicians, and Dr. Jackson was considerably older than his younger colleagues. Almost immediately, Dr. Blake, the visionary, conceived the brilliant idea that he and Dr. Ivey should build and operate their own medical clinic. When approached, Dr. Ivey readily accepted the suggestion, and the two purchased the vacant property in 1982 at the intersection of Lake Wire and Martin Luther King Boulevard in Lakeland.

Fully aware of the thickly overgrown lakefront real estate, my husband loaded our lawnmower into the trunk of his Pontiac and traveled to the site to eliminate the excessive overgrowth of weeds. Throwing caution to the winds, Mark leaned forward in an awkward position to remove the mower, causing serious back injury, and I think he said that it was neurasthenia in his thighs (a mechanical weakness of the nerves), or was it meralgia paresthetica? Anyway, the pain was too severe for him to drive home, but the office was merely blocks away. So, he painfully made the drive and called me.

I successfully got him home and in bed, and I insisted on his visiting an orthopedist, but he refused. “Let’s wait until tomorrow and see,” he begged. I heard the identical refrain for one week, and then I made the suggestion no longer. I instantly called our orthopedist and made and appointment. He was available to see us right away. I dressed him and somehow managed to get him, a man considerably much heavier than I, into the car safely by backing it up to the front entrance as close as possible.

Regrettably, the ride was very uncomfortable for him. His pleasant face responded with a painful grimace with every pothole and slightly raised manhole I hit. I then drove more cautiously to avoid all of them.

When at the doctor’s office, he was physically examined and X-rayed.

I was ordered to take him to the hospital. Once we were in the car, “I can’t go to the hospital,” my hurting husband bemoaned.

“Why?”

“I don’t have a toothbrush, pajamas or anything.”

“I’m taking you to the hospital now and I will return with all of your needs.”

He had no more excuses. I presume some anxiety had been triggered by fear of receiving bad news.

Mark was admitted into the hospital and traction was used for his lumbar spinal disorders. My husband’s recovery was not as swift as I had hoped and thought it should be. I began to stress as I always did. Could it have been some type of cancer? I imagined. I secretly called my friend to voice my concerns. My fear was driving me to be irrational. My telephone call to my friend verified that! “Cancer just doesn’t jump on you like that!” she ardently asserted.

When we arrived in Lakeland, I had decided to take respite from teaching and the numerous hats I had worn, but two incomes were a necessity at this time. While my husband lay in bed, recovering from his injuries, bills started to mount, and we had no idea when he would be able to resume his work. This was one more major concern that increased my anxiety. Later, I learned that he was compensated for patients' visits through insurance filings. Thank God! During his recovery, I drove him to and from the office for a period of time.

All the same, I personally committed to never find ourselves in such a quagmire again. That following summer, I attended a local college and fulfilled all requirements to restart my teaching career in Lakeland, Polk County, Florida. I could not have been more joyful to have been led by the Holy Spirit to have done so.

Chapter 6
The Long Journey to the Great Depression

It was 1985. Mark was about to celebrate his fiftieth birthday. Our one-time family of five now had dwindled to a precious few. Only our youngest son, Mark and I were left. On that morning, we had just finished breakfast. Michael and I sat in silence and watched Dad eagerly swallow exorbitant amounts of water. He, too, promptly observed and acknowledged that he'd had an insatiable thirst for water. He thought for a second and took a minute to test himself for diabetes. When he had finished the test, clearly written in his face was bewildered shock. He apparently thought the test was inaccurate. He repeated the test for a second time and then a third time. It was indisputable! He had developed Type 2 diabetes. This was a gamechanger for all of us, although it was not a death sentence. However, what a challenge this would be! My husband seemed to have a voracious appetite for nearly everything and sweets. Could he modify and moderate his eating habits?

One Sunday, the three of us left church, and in recent years we'd begun to dine out after church services. We all were incessantly ravenous after the two hours, so we drove the eleven-mile trip to Morrison's Cafeteria in Winter Haven, Florida. My husband, who was born and had grown up in the community of Santos, a rural area of Ocala, Marion County, Florida, loved that down-home cooking that consisted of beans, rice, cornbread and almost any fried entree with iced tea, garnished with a lemon wedge. Regularly, when he'd hastily consumed the ice-cold beverage, he'd take the garnishment, firmly squeeze it and add lots of sugar to his glass of water to make lemonade. On this Sunday, however, Mark selected steak as his principal course. We all seemed to be enjoying our meals when I looked up and found that Mark was frozen in one position, no longer eating nor talking. I frantically asked, "What's wrong?!" He could not respond. I panicked and shouted, "I'm calling 911!" while quickly rising from my chair. He quickly grabbed my hand and forced me to sit. I knew this meant just wait a moment. Then, I heard him joyfully say, "It's gone." The steak had become lodged in his esophagus and just stubbornly sat there. I'd never seen that happen before, but I pondered over the number of times this might have happened in the past during my absence.

Sundays offered opportunities for our small family to dine together. Had they not been, I might not have known the recurrence of those episodes that I have now come to know as dysphagia, difficulty in swallowing. We often frequented Red Lobster, one of my favorites. There was another occurrence of my husband's choking. As before, conversation and eating abruptly ceased. Now, whenever he began to experience the difficulty, he unobtrusively rose from his seat and sauntered off to the restroom. He never wanted to attract attention. Forthwith and with deep concern, I'd turn to our son, "Please, go check on your dad," I'd implore. Whenever one of our sons was there, their findings were forever the same. Their father was regurgitating. He had induced regurgitation to alleviate the discomfort or chest pain. In other words, for instant relief he was ejecting the contents of the esophagus that had stuck in his throat. When he had recovered, he would rejoin us at the table and continue the consumption of his meal.

Unfortunately, my husband did not want to visit doctors. I don't know and never knew the reason. Perhaps as a physician he knew what to expect and didn't want to subject himself to the process, which could have resulted in a surgical procedure, but seldom did he have reservation to inform me of some of his minor health issues. Once, as he was readying himself for the office, he called out anxiously to me from the bathroom, "Jack, come here and look at my throat!" He widely opened his mouth toward the light as I peered intently in amazement. His uvula was elongated and sitting on his tongue! This soft tissue functions to block passage into the nasal cavity when one swallows and prevents fluids or foods from entering the nasal passages. I, too, was dressing for work. So I contacted the school administration that I had an emergency and there was a need for a substitute teacher. Then, without further delay, I telephoned the otolaryngologist, a physician who treats the ears, nose and throat (ENT). The ENT saw us immediately. Ultimately, Dr. Aguilera recommended and performed an uvulectomy (removal of the uvula). Mark's weight gain, irregular sleep or both had probably contributed to this condition. Of course, my husband's reticence to visit health providers about his health issues in a timely manner, if at all, were surely heightening my anxiety.

During the summer of 1995, I really felt anxious, especially after learning of a friend's similar problem. I had been communicating with an acquaintance, who'd had unbearable pain resulting from cervical problems. I'm not aware of which condition it might have been, but she offered specific details about the treatment. Her physician elected to perform either anterior cervical or anterior interbody fusion. This is when the surgeon makes an incision from the front of the neck. I could listen to no more. The mere thought of someone opening the front of my neck terrified me. As was a colleague, I had been examined by two different neurologists and had been subjected to the displeasure of the magnetic resonance imaging (MRI). When I saw the second specialist, the MRI indicated that I had cervical damage at the C2 and C3 junctions. This meant that I could have limited mobility in both flexion and extension. Flexion is the movement of the chin toward the chest and extension is the backward movement of the head. The neurologist did not reveal my high blood pressure levels, but he adamantly said, "I don't want you to have a stroke!" My pressure most assuredly had crept up. At any rate, he highly recommended that I see a local license massage therapist (LMT). He favorably added, "She's the best I've ever seen!"

When I had lain down for bed that night, I was severely impacted by the visual effects of the colleague's accounts of her surgical treatment and could not efface them. I lay there, and I felt prickling sensations in my legs. The longer I lay there, the more intense became the irritation. What was happening to me?!

I had made an appointment with the LMT, whom my neurologist had given an excellent review. She held me at her office, treating my issues, guiding and teaching me how to alleviate pain and prevent injuries, far beyond the hour for which I was guaranteed and for which I had paid. The prickling ceased and all evidence of cervical injury faded when she successfully treated the cervical issues that Dr. Cuervo had diagnosed. It was clear that my husband's lack to care for his physical health in a timely manner, or if at all, was negatively affecting his health and mine.

Chapter 7
TIA -The Mini Stroke

It was sometime during the mid-nineties. My husband related to me that while at the hospital, one of the obstetric nurses had noticed his right hand was slightly larger than his left. At some point, my husband recognized there was a permanent tingling in his right hand. Though affected, he had not realized he had had a cerebrovascular accident (CVA), commonly known as a stroke. Perhaps it was a transient ischemic attack (TIA). A transient ischemic attack might last only for an hour but seldom up to twenty-four hours. The persistent effect of the mini-stroke necessitated his wearing an edema glove for his swollen hand.

We would have been married for thirty-eight years on June 15, 1995, and the Annual National Medical Association Convention (NMA) was to be held in Los Angeles, California. I had always enjoyed and greatly anticipated the planned activities that involved the physicians' spouses for each day of the convention. So I continuously accompanied Mark to each one. To my surprise, my loving husband had orchestrated plans for us to board a flight to Oahu, the third-largest island in Hawaii, to celebrate our anniversary after the convention. I was extremely enthusiastic but to some degree troubled since he had strongly complained of a nagging toothache that he would endure while in Hawaii. I worried that there was an urgent need to see a dentist, but he insisted on our romantic getaway.

The following day, he did not appear to be quite himself. There clearly was a noticeable decline in Mark's health. His regular and moderate gait had become slower and more labored as we walked the streets of Honolulu, a city of about one-half million people. Having toured the Big Island, Honolulu truly was the more beautiful of the two islands. Anyway, as we walked along the streets of this capital city, I was taken in by the breathtaking flora. A tour guide had earlier informed us that the plants had come from other places either by the birds, winds or people, and there were the skyscrapers of this metropolitan city. I suddenly realized I was so captivated by this city's charm that I'd left my love behind. He could no longer keep pace with me. Spending entire nights and days with my husband permitted me to more closely observe his gradual declivity, and this was daunting for me.

When we returned to Florida, Mark saw a dentist to treat his dental issues. The dental hygienist began with the cleaning of his teeth as well. Oh, but was he furious! He was certain the hygienist had used the scaler to remove plaque from his teeth too far beneath the gumline and his entire mouth was sore. Perhaps this was his hesitancy to see medical and dental professionals, but I knew that with all of the pain he had endured he was no weakling. Perhaps he disliked sharp instruments.

Near the end of the 1990s, I could not have fathomed what would happen next! To our chagrin, my husband and I were ousted from our local church. As staunch members and supporters of our church, I was overwhelmed with grief and disappointment. However, I had grown weary of the constant browbeating. My weekly visits to church were to worship God, fellowship with other congregants and self-edify. My husband and I had visited another church probably twice when the bad-tempered behavior from the pulpit became too extreme. I soon was informed that our names were removed from the church's roll, not by the church but a friend. Unfortunately, she and her spouse received the identical penalty as did a few others. If it were true, how frivolous and unchristian! I was incapable to surmount the hill of difficulties. My husband had developed diabetes and acid reflux, and he'd had a mini-stroke, and then we both were ostracized from the church. Anxiety was taking full control of my life. In addition to the chest pains, fluttery stomach, hypertension, neck and back pain I'd developed, my hands had become bubble wrap, blistery. I was obsessed with the thought that I could lose my husband and neither of us would have a church to call home. By this time, it was evident that I had crossed the threshold of trepidation. Those protrusions that resembled bubble wrap were clear, watery blisters that had formed between every finger and on the palms of both my hands, that seemed to come from nowhere. They were not infected, did not hurt, itch, leak, nor did they drain on their own. Nervously, I pinched and burst each of them, but others would appear. There was an urgent need to consult a dermatologist. "Are you allergic to latex?" he asked. No, I was not. I was given a topical lotion to use on the affected areas. Stress had led to those conditions because I hadn't fully learned how to relinquish my "what ifs," fears and anxieties and cast them on Him.

I know that God knows what fear does to His children. That's why Paul tells us in Philippians 4:6, "Do not be anxious about anything, but in everything by prayer and supplication with thanksgiving let your requests be made known to God" (ESV). Paul's promise is that those things would positively affect the emotional, mental, physical and spiritual health upon the children of God. Why did I not believe beyond a doubt that my God shall supply all my needs according to His riches in glory by Christ Jesus?" (Philippians 4:19)

I was thoroughly preoccupied with Mark's health issues. My fear was that his health problems would lead to my being alone since all of our nestlings had taken the big leap. I had given my heart to him, this gift from God, so many decades ago. He was my first and only true love. He was always patient, kind, respectful, smart, supportive, the epitome of sangfroid and a loving husband and father. He, too, had a great sense of humor and leadership skills. I knew 2 Timothy 1:7 says, "For God has not given us a spirit of fear, but of power and of love and of a sound mind," but I was powerless to let go. It was indisputable in my mind that if I lost Mark, there would be a permanent hurdle in my life, and I knew that I was incapable of crossing it and loving that way ever again.

Once more, one early morning I was preparing to leave for school. My husband cried out to me to take a look at his leg. He raised his pant leg. His skin was mottled all over—blotchy in appearance with red spots. I was astounded and confounded. Never had I seen this condition. I instantaneously telephoned our close friend, who was an internist, and gave an accurate description of what I had observed. Dr. Rudolph Dorsett advised me to take him to the hospital, where he met us. He was seen in the emergency room and hospitalized for several days before his release. I still do not know the diagnosis, but the mottling had completely disappeared and could have occurred for a number of reasons.

Chapter 8
The Effects of Diabetes

Regrettably, there was no deceleration in Mark's mounting physical ailments, nor my anxiety.

After dinner, he often had sat, watched television or listened to jazz, one of his hobbies. Jazz was not now a preference as much as before. He'd started to come to bed earlier, and I'd begun to hear a frightening cough whenever he had lain down in bed during my many restless nights. By this time, I'd learned to make a dash for the plastic-lined trashcan that sat in the master bathroom. The cough had been triggered when some acidic contents of his stomach reentered his esophagus. I held the trashcan beneath his head so that the semi-digested food would issue from his mouth into the plastic. When he'd finished, I'd tie the top of the plastic liner and dispose of its contents.

I'd seen this scene played over so often that I cringed each time I heard footsteps in the dark just before a full figure filled the doorway and Mark's entrance into our bedroom. I recall many times earlier I'd humbly begged him to come to bed and suggested he might want to slip out when I'd fallen asleep. I had yearned to be next to him, but now I had dreaded what might happen when we were alone together in bed.

My intense fears were not for naught. My husband often saw patients and did not regularly stop for a lunch break. This would cause his sugar levels to drop. Once, I saw him pull up in the driveway and waited to hear the key turn in the door of the laundry room. After checking several times, *Maybe he was speaking with our neighbor,* I thought. I gave him sufficient time before walking outside to confirm my thoughts. There he was slumped over the steering wheel! He'd never exited the car! I quickly flung the door open, awoke and assisted him inside. He was utterly confused. Thanks to a gracious God that this did not occur in the midst of the heavy evening traffic.

That would not be the last for such an unsettling reality. Besides his own private practice, Mark was employed one day of the week as a physician at a drug rehabilitation center in Polk County when his office was closed. It was late afternoon when I received a critical call that my husband was found unconscious at his desk. An ambulance was dispatched, and he was expressed to the hospital. I often wondered if he were aware of the symptoms of his hypoglycemia, for I had constantly monitored and recognized the signs of his low blood sugar levels: clamminess of hands and arms, inability to think clearly and a slow response or no response. In a class for Type 2 diabetic patients, and one that my husband taught as well, we were instructed to always have some kind of sugary food at hand. Drink four ounces of orange juice or pop, eat a small piece of hard candy or jelly to counteract the risks of hypoglycemia.

I can't forget that Lord's Day following church services when Mark and I went to Red Lobster for dinner. The server promptly approached us at our table, welcomed us and inquired, "Would you like to continue to look at the menu, or are you ready to order?" kindly with a smile. We ordered and sat and chatted for a short period. Initially, I thought my husband was listening and simply wearing a broad smile when his expression did not change. I quickly stepped down from the high-top table and grasped his hand and arm. Both were extremely clammy. I frantically requested orange juice. Our server suggested we remove him from the high table and lay him on the floor. Someone had requested an ambulance. By the time of its arrival, Mark had successfully devoured the juice. One of the emergency medical technicians informed him that they were there to transport him to the hospital. "I'm not going to the hospital!" he exclaimed hotly. The EMT pointed directly at me and inquired of him, "Who is that?" "That's my wife?!" he said decisively and with a tone that suggested the EMT was a few knives short of a table setting. He stood up, paid for our meals and we left, finding his way down the many steps and to our automobile before driving away.

I am grateful to God that we were together that day and for all the times prior to and following, but perpetually worried about his operating a vehicle alone. He was somewhat stubborn and often neglected the important steps to avoid hypoglycemia, for there is a definitive difference between faith and folly. I was never efficient to ascertain if he were capable of recognizing threatening signs of unconsciousness that could result in death.

Chapter 9
The Great Depression

With all of my husband's health problems growing incrementally, I most assuredly knew the worst would happen. I'd begun to have unexplained headaches that became so severe that I had to vacate my teaching position during the day at times to visit the doctor's office. After several appointments, I was prescribed a medication for the evening for insomnia and another that was to be taken in the morning to avoid prolonged drowsiness so that I could more capably begin a new day. After a few weeks of this insanity, I refused to swallow another pill.

One morning, I recall standing in the hallway at the school where I was employed, having a brief conversation with a paraprofessional who'd said that a colleague's father had passed. I instantly lost strength in my legs and could no longer stand. I asked for a chair from a nearby classroom and sat while trying to regain the firmness to stand and return to my classroom. I knew her father had been hospitalized for a very short period of time, and I'd prayed for her mother even though I could not pray for myself. How ironic! I had also recalled that our colleague had related to me that her family had not known that her father had acquired diabetes. The news of this man's death only exacerbated my symptoms of depression. I had had another panic attack, for "it was a surety my husband's days on this earth were short!" I mused.

At my follow-up appointment, the doctor's assistant entered the examination room and took my blood pressure. I asked, "What is it?" She began to stammer, even though she was not a stutterer. "I-I-I d-don't know! The d-doctor will have to check it." When he had taken my pressure, I asked with much concern, "What is it?" I recalled the systolic pressure number was over 250 and the diastolic pressure number was over 100. The doctor turned to me and he removed his sphygmomanometer (blood pressure monitor) and said, "I'm afraid you're going to have a stroke." I grew faint even more. I was given nitroglycerin to place beneath my tongue. This medication breaks down into nitric oxide, which causes the smooth muscle within the blood vessels to relax. As a result, the arteries and veins open up, permitting additional blood to flow through. So I learned that nitroglycerin is used to lower the blood pressure as well as treat the heart.

With the passing of each new day and no options for treatment to combat those feelings of intense worry, nor preparation to face those fears, I was rapidly losing all control. Heretofore, I had greatly enjoyed teaching and looked forward to it daily, now even more so because it was a diversion. It pulled my attention away from the anxious thoughts of ultimately burying my husband. So I coped pretty well at school until Friday afternoon, an hour before school dismissal. But now, the last workday of the week would compel me to spend the next two days entirely alone with Mark and his increasing list of health problems. At this point, I'd become exceedingly nauseous. Accompanying my other symptoms of anxiety, I could add nausea and regurgitation. Once at home, I lay in bed only moments before I could no longer keep my digestive system intact. I stumbled to the bathroom just in time while heaving and vomiting. When Mark arrived from the office, I had only been capable of closing and locking the doors to our home. Now the roles were reversed. He was caring for me.

The next week, my anxiety elevated even more. I had grown fearful to see Thursday since Friday followed. That meant I would have to spend another weekend with my "dying" husband, and this was simply too much to bear. Tears were no outlet, but I could no longer retain them. This pattern of regretting the dawn of a new day and being alone with my husband continued. I was acutely uneasy to see Wednesday, for there would be just two days prior to the weekend. The anticipation of each new day became so unbearably torturous that I hadn't the strength anymore to cast one leg over the side of the bed to drag my body up. My arms had become limp, too weak to raise them to pull a comb through my hair, brush my teeth or take a bath. I knew nutrition was important, but every bite was like sinking my teeth into sawdust. I could not eat anything, and my eyes were repositories of tears that freely rushed down my cheeks each day. I'd read the Bible three times, from the Old and through the New Testaments, but I could not pray, read a Scripture or recall one—no, not one! I could not watch television, nor hold a conversation. I could no longer concentrate, and my attention span was of no value.

One weekend, one of our sons had said that he'd bring his two young daughters to visit while he was on his way to Tampa. I found so much joy in knowing those sweet little granddaughters would be spending meeting and powwow time with "nana." We would go to McDonald's and spend a few fun and playful hours together. This would be another diversion from my anxiety. They arrived in the evening. "Nana" was beyond excited to see them, but the pinnacle of enthusiasm grew old quickly. I could not drive to the fast-food restaurant. They were too talkative, a ton of questions, and too active. I had immediately wondered, "Where is their father? Please come get them!" There was absolutely nothing I could do to temper the out-of-control anxiety. I could not scratch my way up from the depths of that black ruinous hole.

When I had finally garnered enough strength to rise from my bed, I found myself teetering on the edge of an abyss. So I ambled up to my bedroom window to view creation on the other side of the Plexiglas. A bright yellow sun's brilliant rays had burst through the white fluffy clouds and slowly drifted across the pale blue expanse.

Colorful birds sang from their little hearts cheerful melodies from their perches and some while in flight. Flowers' sweet fragrant aromas wafted through the morning air, and the sounds of children were a symphony of laughter and play. My physical eyes had seen God's wondrous creation, but in my mind's eye there was merely dread, darkness that was blacker than a thousand midnights and deafening silence.

I had lain in bed, powerless to leave my bedroom all weekend and then for the weeks that followed, except for doctor's appointments. My bedroom had become my refuge. If only I could have remembered that "God is our refuge and strength, a very present help in trouble" (Psalm 46:1). Although fear is a natural emotion and survival skill, it can impact one's mental and physical health negatively at times when it warns to respond to danger by fight or flight when one feels threatened, and it is imperative to remember that God said He would be with us. Retrospectively, I wish I had not so proudly portrayed myself as "Superwoman," a wise, strong, confident, go-it-alone kind of woman. Instead, I wish I had put my trust in the Lord with all my heart. After the weekend, it was quite apparent that I could not return to school on that following Monday. I'd found myself in a bigger and deeper black hole, distressed and utterly helpless. Fear and stress had been manifested in numerous ways over a period of time by now: Watery blisters had once formed on my hands, and I nervously pinched and burst each one before I was prescribed medication for that condition. I became incessantly lachrymose and developed hypertension, severe headaches, prickling of the legs, neck and back pain, loss of appetite, vomiting, a short attention span, insomnia sometimes and hypersomnia at other times, nausea and depression that I would never want for my worst enemy. I had tried clawing my way toward the top, always losing my footing and slipping away once again.

I could not *will* myself out of the grips of this great depression. I knew it was imperative that I seek help. I carelessly grabbed the

Lakeland Telephone Directory and ripped through the pages frantically to find a psychiatrist, one whom I could see for the many levels of depression I was experiencing. I instantly called the first one I'd found. An appointment was not available for two weeks. The wait was too long! I searched for another and scheduled an appointment that was a week away. I hadn't that much time, so I called back and canceled. I made still a third call and I could be seen immediately, but then I was told, "Wait just a minute," and I was placed on hold. When the receptionist returned, she said, "There's a red flag. Let me call you back." I tried to be patient as I waited until the next day. Desperate for an answer, I telephoned the third office again, and once more I was told about *that* red flag. I could no longer bridle my temperament. "I need help!" I shouted loudly into the telephone. "Oh, yes, ma'am, we can see you tomorrow morning." I was pretty sure that she had concluded that the outcome would not be good if I hadn't gotten help instantly.

The appointed day came when I would see the psychiatrist for the chronic anxiety and depression that had constantly plagued me. Nonetheless, I was keenly aware that I had to gather my wits to dress and go in order to improve my health. I still could not comb my hair nor bathe, but I brushed my teeth, wrapped my hair in a scarf and carelessly dressed before driving to the Watson Clinic.

After disembarkation of my vehicle at the clinic, I walked nervously up to the receptionist, who passed several sheets of forms to me to be completed. I clenched them with trembling hands, found a chair and sank in it. I could barely steady my quiver. I looked up curiously to see if others were behaving similarly. They weren't.

If this had been a test from God, I had failed it miserably. Christians know that God tests His children's faith. In Genesis 22, God tested Abraham when He told him to take his son, Isaac, to the region of Moriah and sacrifice him as a burnt offering on one of the mountains. Abraham was obedient, taking his son, wood he'd cut for the burnt offering, and a knife. He placed the wood on his son, Isaac.

The son asked his father about the lamb that was to be sacrificed. "The fire and wood are here," Abraham answered. "But where is the lamb for the sacrificial offering?" Isaac asked. "God will provide the lamb and the burnt offering, my son," Abraham replied. Isaac had no idea that God was asking Abraham to place him on the altar to be sacrificed, but before Abraham could slay his bound son, who lay on the altar, God said to him, "Do not lay a hand on the boy. Do not do anything to him. Now that I know you fear God because you have not withheld him from Me, your son, your only son." When Abraham looked up, he saw a ram caught in the thicket by its horns. Abraham then sacrificed the ram. Surely, Abraham was a holy man of faith. He trusted God wholeheartedly. (Genesis 22:1-19)

There were many others in the Bible who were tested as well. God tested Job when He allowed Satan to attack his health, take away his family and all for which he had labored to have (Job 2). Shadrach, Meshach, and Abednego were tested (Daniel 3), as were many others. According to Tom Shepard's *Seven Examples of Testing in the Bible* (October 30, 2006), God continually tests people's character, faith, obedience, love, integrity and loyalty.

At any rate, the psychiatrist's diagnosis for me was one of clinical depression, and her first inclination was to hospitalize me, but instead I was treated and prescribed an antidepressant for this mental disorder. I was given an appointment to visit the counselor every other day for the next three weeks and the psychiatrist intermittently. I was told that I was seen as often as I was to prepare me to return to my work because they both had seen my intense effort to lift the veil of darkness that enveloped my whole being.

As I remained at home, trying to escape the ferocious pull of that black hole, I was showered with love. There were telephone calls, food, prayers and gifts of books. With the exception of doctor's visits, I had not been able to leave my bedroom. I gradually took steps beyond my bedroom door when a prayer partner and friend insisted on my taking an automobile ride. This, too, was wisely advised by my counselor. She had recommended small steps toward my journey to success. Capable of some television programming, I watched only Christian networks and programs, and they all seemed to speak to me. I began to learn verses of Holy Scripture on God's promises in the book of the same name that was gifted to me. I could pray again, and three weeks later I was healthy enough to teach again. Friends are valuable.

According to the Word of God, "A friend is always a friend and relatives are born to share our troubles" (Proverbs 17:17).

After three weeks of recovering, with prayer, reading and learning Scriptures, counseling, antidepressant medication to regulate brain chemistry and God's amazing grace, I was blessed and thankful to return to my classroom. There was definite healing in hearing and reading God's Word, especially this verse from 3 John 1:2, "Beloved, I wish above all things that thou mayest prosper and be in health, even as thy soul prospereth." I repeated that verse daily, among many others, until they were etched on my heart.

Chapter 10
Mark's Brain Infarction – The Big Stroke

By this time, I'd grown fairly accustomed to but not comfortable with our very efficient secretary using the school intercom system to ask me to pick up an incoming phone call in the teachers' workroom, which was right across the hallway from my classroom. My husband's colleague was calling, "Jackie, we found Mark passed out at his desk and he isn't responding. The ambulance has taken him to Lakeland Regional Medical Center." When I shared this information with the secretary, the tenderhearted Mrs. Sanders suggested, "Mrs. Ivey, don't worry about anything. We'll take care of everything for you, and we'll get someone to cover your class," she sympathized.

I hurried to be at my husband's bedside. One of my fears had been realized. He'd been diagnosed with a cerebral infarction, or stroke, a condition caused by a sudden loss of oxygen to the brain. It is my understanding that millions of people suffer from them yearly, and nearly half of them do not survive. At any rate, when I saw my husband I stepped outside of his room, for tears flooded my eyes and washed down my face. I could not bear to see him in that condition. Moreover, I did not know if I could survive if he were to pass away. Thank God, he did not die, nor did he have severe disabilities!

After a few weeks in the intensive care unit (ICU) and a stay in a private medical room in the hospital, my husband was to transition from the hospital to rehabilitation, where the program was extremely aggressive. However, it had been determined that Mark had dysphagia, a disorder of swallowing safely. He would not be permitted to eat until deemed safe by the speech pathologist. As a result, a feeding tube was recommended and inserted so that his nutritional needs were met.

I was permitted to drive him since he refused to be transported by ambulance. After weeks in that hospital, he was excited to ride in his own vehicle and revel in God's presence through sights and sounds of His creation and feel a soft, fresh breeze gently sweep against his skin. I had often wheeled him through the hospital corridors and in the hospital yard, but this was a car ride through streets very much unlike a wheelchair.

We arrived at the rehabilitation center at the hospital, which was eleven miles away, and my husband was checked in and received a room. I stayed with him until dusk because I wanted to be at home as near to nightfall as possible, and there was school for me the next day.

When it was time to leave, I could barely tear myself away. If anyone could imagine the difficulty in abandoning your infant, that is how heart-wrenching that was for me. Anyway, my darling worked indefatigably in each category of his therapy to regain functionality. He had lost some dexterity and strength in his left hand and mobility in his left leg. In addition to physical therapy, there were occupational and speech therapies. Needless to say, he would not return to his practice ever again. The brain attack forced him into an early retirement in 1999.

Chapter 11
Mark's Undiagnosed Acid Reflux

That frightening cough that had begun earlier, whenever he had lain down in bed, had begun to be more frequent, but when I then heard it I was quick to be of assistance to him, but no more did I panic. Nonetheless, I was vastly affected about this ongoing problem. I held the trashcan each time beneath his head so that the semi-digested food would gush from his mouth into the plastic bag. When he'd finished, again I'd tie the top of the plastic liner and disposed of its contents. This scenario was consistently duplicated. Mark had not seen a gastroenterologist, a doctor who treats problems and diseases of the digestive system and is an expert in how the digestive system works. I straightaway made an appointment for him. We were advised that an endoscopy would be necessary to diagnose the problem, and we were given specific instructions that all eating and/or drinking must be discontinued at least eight hours prior to the procedure.

Since it was a necessity that my husband be sedated during the procedure and would not be able to drive himself back home because of the lingering effects of the anesthesia, I took the day off to drive him to the hospital as an outpatient and waited anxiously for the results of the test. When the endoscopy was completed, I was led from the waiting room into the recovery room and shown the images of the cancer that the endoscope or camera had captured. Mark had been diagnosed with gastroesophageal junction cancer. This kind of cancer for him affected the lower part of the esophagus, or the place where the esophagus and stomach meet, which is known as the gastroesophageal, or GE junction. Yes, cancer was the culprit! That was the reason for my husband's constant regurgitation. Prior to the cancer, he was suffering from acid reflux. Why didn't my husband, the medical doctor, take care of himself?! Acid reflux was such an easy fix and commonplace among many individuals. Many people suffer from this condition, that very distasteful burning sensation that occurs in the chest, commonly referred to as heartburn. He always reminded me of pap smears, mammograms, endoscopies and colonoscopies and anything medical. Cancer had been my greatest fear! It had been the cause of death of my mother, one of my uncles and a cousin at that time. Nonetheless, Mark's primary physician referred us to an oncologist.

When we visited with the oncologist to explore our options, he first recommended an esophagectomy. The surgeon would remove part of the stomach and part of the esophagus, only the affected or cancerous areas, but he knew of no one who could perform this surgery locally; so we were referred to a surgeon in Tampa, Florida. We both sat and listened to the method of the procedure, which would involve the stomach being connected to the remainder of the esophagus. That possibly could have placed the stomach high in the chest. Mark had had a stroke, but there was no brain injury and he was still a physician.

When we had left the doctor's office, my sweetheart turned to me and said with much resolution, "I'm not going to let anyone put my stomach in my chest!!" So he refused that treatment and opted for chemotherapy and radiation. He received chemotherapy and radiation as treatment, but the side-effect of nausea and vomiting was vicious. I can recall once erring while driving the two of us to Tampa's International Mall, unequipped to handle those two of the side-effects. Mark loved getting out of the house, so I took him with me always, except to work. Two outstanding and capable caregivers were hired to care for his needs during that time. They, too, would take him on joy rides and report how he stared out of the car window, enjoying the sights and sounds. Though it has been said that one of the side-effects of radiation is loss of hair, he never lost any. Never once during his illness did he complain or moan, so it was difficult to know if he were ever tired. He continually demonstrated a cheerful spirit. This was he, never wanting to ruffle me or cause consternation, but he had. It was the great depression! I simply had not revealed it to him even though he'd asked me numerous times why I was crying. Once, before his stroke, he'd decided he would not go into the office but stay with me. I encouraged him to see his patients. We were two faithful, loving spirits, engaged in trying to protect and take care of each other.

Chapter 12
The Return of the Cancer and Another Brain Infarction

About 2001, we learned that the gastroesophageal, or GE junction cancer had returned. This was a troublesome revelation to receive, but I endured. However, my psychiatrist had previously increased by medication dosage of the antidepressant by 10 milligrams. Most importantly, I was reading God's Word and had accumulated countless verses of Scripture that were most certainly comforting. What privileges and promises we have as believers in Christ Jesus. According to the Apostle Paul, it is God "who comforts us in all our affliction, so that we may be able to comfort those who are in any affliction, with the comfort with which we ourselves are comforted by God" (2 Corinthians 1:4). Suffering is often compared to the refining of an impure metal. The silversmith takes a piece of silver, holds it over the middle of the fire at the place that it is hottest, and always keeps his eye on the silver until the dross or impurities are burned away. He knows that it's fully refined when he sees his image in the piece (Mark Batterson: *Primal*). We can read in Proverbs 25:4, and there are many more Scriptures to see that God uses this process to refine His children. He uses hardships, difficult circumstances and suffering to refine us into His Son's image. I was sure I had gone through the fire and was much better for it. My suffering was representative of the fire, which God allowed. I thought I had been held there until my fears, anxieties and panic attacks ceased. Had all the impurities been removed? Nonetheless, I was sure that I had emerged a changed person and better prepared to comfort others. Unquestionably, I was equipped to accept the ghastly news of the recurrence of the cancer.

In the meantime, Michael, our youngest son, had come home again to visit with his ailing father. I'd left early in the morning to report to my work, but it was in the afternoon when I heard the quiet opening of the door to my classroom. Mrs. Sanders was standing there. I just knew there was distressing news. Her mere presence was indicative of that by now. Seemingly, she had created every innovative method possible to communicate with me whenever a telephone call came from my home without alarming me. This practice was now customary, and I was and am eternally grateful for her prudence. Anyway, my husband's caregiver was on the line. I hesitantly picked up the phone and Freddie, the caregiver, was worried and perplexed that "Dr. Ivey" was uninterested in eating the meal I had prepared before I'd left. I must insert that he was blessed and we were thankful that his feeding tube had been removed much earlier. I feared his blood sugar level might drop to a dangerous level. So I promised I'd be coming home, but before I could hang up, "Mom, Mom, does Dad always look at you like this?" my son asked frantically. He tried to explain the strange look on his dad's face that he was seeing. "I don't know what you're talking about, but I'm coming home," I answered. As usual, Mrs. Sanders promised to and responded to my needs again so that I was free to leave my classroom.

When I arrived home and parked my car, I rushed through the door that led into the laundry room and then to my husband, who was sitting in the family room. He appeared to have a smile on his face that could not be erased. I gently touched his hands and arms and they were warm and clammy. I was pretty sure he was becoming hypoglycemic, the dropping of one's blood sugar level. I reached out to assist him in the rise from the rather low chair. My first thought was to raise his blood sugar level and give him a bath, but there was something terribly wrong that I hadn't experienced before. Without delay, I blurted, "I'm calling the ambulance!" I raced to the telephone and called 911. Within minutes, the paramedics were there. My beloved was having another stroke. He was transported to the hospital in a coma.

I must always thank my Father for giving them both the presence of mind to closely observe and make known their findings.

At this point, I could not fully understand why all the need for additional suffering. I started to think back over my life and tried to recall all the wrong I'd done. There was a certainty that I was being punished because in my mind, for every action there is a consequence. No, that was not it! Perhaps my faith was continually being tested. I had recalled that God uses suffering as an instrument to grow us, His children, to mold, strengthen and teach us. He disciplines us as we might discipline our children. It's an act of love. Isn't this the reason for chastising our children? Our children are gifts from God and He says that children are to obey their parents in the Lord because this is right. They are to honor their father and mother that it may go well with them so that they may live long in the land (Ephesians 6:1-3). We are God's children by adoption and He wants us to be obedient children as well. So affliction, suffering, trials and the like are tools to help mold us into His image. Charles Spurgeon said, "They who dive in the sea of affliction bring up rare pearls." I continued to have concerns and worries, but not as before. I had grown, but this was not the end of the process. God is always the determinant.

Again in the intensive care unit, we visited Mark, my comatose husband. Upon notification, a friend of Michael's drove from Atlanta alone to be with us amid another dark period of our lives. So did friends from Chicago, Illinois. I saw my husband twice daily, but we all visited him daily and surrounded his bed and prayed incessantly for the week that he lay comatose, in that state of unconsciousness with minimal brain activity and hooked up to a ventilator. The stroke-induced coma and his medical issues had caused breathing on his own difficult. Thus, a ventilator was necessary. One day during that week, our son Michael had whispered into his dad's ear while holding his hand, "Dad, if you can hear me, squeeze my hand." A smile spread across Michael's face when he felt his dad's fingers tightening around his. We were astonished but oh, so filled with gratitude! By His grace, our sovereign Father had bestowed our husband and father another opportunity to continue this life's journey. To God be the glory!

Mark's physician was making his rounds when he walked into the ICU room, where we stood, to find this small group of family surrounding and hovering over my beloved's bed. We exchanged pleasantries, and he proceeded to check Mark's medical chart for new entries that his healthcare team might have included, such as consults, flowcharts, progress and/or test results. During this time my husband, awake now, gestured and grunted that he wanted the ventilator removed. The doctor replied, "If I remove it, will you promise not to remove your IV?" Mark nodded his head with a yes. Soon, the breathing tube that had been inserted in his throat was removed, and he was later transferred to a private room. This was a step up and a step closer to his homecoming, but there would be a transfer to rehabilitation at same hospital first as before.

My beloved was not so enthusiastic as he'd been before. He was uninterested in participating in the rehabilitation program. I was contacted to have him moved to a room, and this was because the hospital's program was much too aggressive for him. I was terribly disappointed. If he were going to be merely a patient, he could have remained in Lakeland at our local hospital. I implored, "Please give him another opportunity. I'll talk with him." They acquiesced and I was very much obliged. However, the extended period of time was extremely brief.

Some days following, I left school to visit my sweetie, the patient, as I'd done tens of times before. He was not in the room, where I'd last seen him in the hospital rehabilitation facility. I inquired to locate his whereabouts. He'd been ejected from the rehabilitation center and transferred to the first floor as a medical patient. I was so, so disappointed and distressed, then angry and pained when I pulled back the bed covers that revealed an expansive wet blood-stained spot that appeared to have been the result of someone who had attempted to insert a catheter by force and had not used a lubricating jelly. Maybe someone didn't care! I don't know the reason, but tears welled up in my eyes, for I could not have imagined the pain that my sweet husband had to tolerate and no one to speak for him. As his advocate, he depended solely on me to assist him in the navigation of the healthcare system. How could I have allowed this to happen? Nonetheless, I was resolved to never see my darling in a predicament such as that again. Without any hesitation, I telephoned Mark's primary physician, and we arranged for my husband's transferal to our local hospital. I thank my heavenly Father that He gave me the presence of mind to be vigilant. I had always been careful and specific to observe him for pressure injuries or decubitus ulcers, and he always told the nurses kindly, "My wife will bathe me." Mark remained in that facility until he was transferred to rehabilitation at a nursing facility.

When Mark was released, my heart overflowed with joy as I brought him to our home again. I found extreme fulfillment in serving and caring for my husband. Of course, caregivers were with him to assist in his needs while I was at work. One son thought it to be monetarily sound to have one of his brothers, who was in the best position to help with the care of their father, return home to help with their dad. So Mark IV and Michael brought their brother Marlon to Lakeland from Fort Lauderdale, Florida. Unfamiliar with the measure his dad could do for himself, Mark fell and was sorely injured. Marlon said nothing because he was unaware of the damage that was sustained. However, the caregiver quickly realized my beloved was in acute pain whenever she touched or moved him and immediately informed me when I returned from school. That necessitated another transport to the hospital by ambulance. The orthopedic physician examined him, and X-rays or imaging tests indicated Mark had endured a hip fracture when he fell. The injury was repaired with surgery and rehabilitation, and of course medication was prescribed for pain. At no time was he in rehabilitation under thirty days subsequent to that injury.

The day that he was discharged from rehabilitation services, I was there to bring him home and most delighted to do so. At this time, we were entering Advent Season. As usual, I was to prepare dinner for Christmas and invite a few close relatives. On Christmas Day, the table had been set the day before with beautiful Lenox Holiday China, napkins, stemware, silverware, place cards, and a beautiful floral arrangement was the centerpiece. After prayer, each person served himself at the Christmas buffet. In the meantime, Marlon had stolen a way and later returned to the dining area with his well-groomed father, whom he had shaved, cut his hair, dressed and then pulled him up to the table to join us as we ate. Although the G tube, or gastronomy tube, was still inserted in his abdomen following the stroke, he had been disconnected from the feeding machine that held a large bag of Glucerna, a high-protein meal that resembles a shake. As Mark sat next to Michael at the dining table with us, he was relaxed and comfortable. While engaged in conversation, he lively chatted while flagrantly taking a piece of cornbread from his son's plate. "Dad, that's mine!" Michael shouted. "Oh, it is? I'm sorry, son," as he continued to take bites and swallow. We knew then that he could eat without aspirating. The food that he'd swallowed did not enter his airway or his lungs. My immediate concern was that he had not been cleared to eat solid food since the second brain infarction, and he should not have eaten the tiniest morsel until his doctor had determined he was stable and healthy enough to take in nutrition and hydration through regular eating and drinking. Anyway, when the dust had settled we tossed our heads back in loud laughter. There was the evidence that God will never leave nor forsake us! He provides pleasure even in the midst of pain and suffering.

Why did I question my suffering? The Word of God tells us that Jesus, our Savior, was born of the Virgin Mary. He was the perfect and spotless lamb of God. Yet He suffered! He was rejected, despised, betrayed, and His face was spat upon. Roman soldiers laughed, smote, slapped and mocked Him as crowds looked on. He was tested, charged, tried and convicted for claiming to be the Son of God. He was stripped of His robe and forced to put on His own clothes. Jesus was tortured, scourged with leather cords, sheep bones, and pieces of metal that were wrapped throughout the cords. While being beaten, pieces of His flesh were ripped away by the large pieces of metal and bone that cut through with every lash before He would leave a bloody trail to be crucified. He would be forced to wear a crown of thorns that scraped His head. His bloody, battered body was now ready for crucifixion. (John 19) Why not me? Why not Me?! I do not expect to be, nor can anyone be above the Master who bore many stripes. No one escapes earth without trials and tribulations. There's suffering because God wants our faith to grow in the face of adversity.

"I was brought forth in iniquity, and in sin did my mother conceive me" (Psalm 51:5). I was born a sinner, but now saved by God's grace and by His stripes. Suffering is purposeful. God has a plan and purpose for all of His children. Jesus Christ came to set me, a sinner, free from the law of sin and death. The perfect lamb of God's righteousness was imputed to my account. The power of sin is lost! Now a lost sinner is saved because Jesus became the propitiation for my sin. This is true for all who believe. Samuel Rutherford (1600-1661), one of the most influential Scottish Presbyterians in the Westminster Assembly, I think said it best, "You cannot be above your Master who received many an innocent stroke." Pastor David McWilliams, Senior Pastor of Covenant Presbyterian Church of

Lakeland, Florida, has said many times, "The Lord sands, polishes and makes us to be who He'll have us be." We all must know the tough paper that we call sandpaper is coated with an abrasive material such as silica, garnet, silicon carbide, or aluminum oxide, that is used to smooth and polish. This has to be painful, thus the suffering. Although there would be no end to Mark's and my suffering, I was better equipped, by God's grace, to cope more easily, for there was much more suffering on this journey. Mark did rather well for months at home. The gastronomy tube had been removed because the doctor had determined he could swallow without aspirating. He particularly enjoyed the taste of food again, and he would sit in our Rattan padded swivel chair and swing his feet from side to side whenever he consumed his favorite fare.

Since my husband experienced such pleasure in eating, I became deeply troubled when his desire for food began to diminish and so had conversations. I recognized he was depressed. Prior to and even during his long illness, he'd always been quite humorous. I spoke to his primary provider regarding his lack of interest in some activities that once were near to his heart. He recognized the depression as well and prescribed an antidepressant. Anyway, one early morning we were lying in bed together when I heard a frightful cough that was similar to the ones I'd recognized from the past. I raced to our master bathroom to retrieve the lined trashcan to catch the contents from his vomiting. There was mere blood. At once, I dialed 911 and summoned an ambulance. Within minutes, the paramedics were at the front door. I led them to our bedroom, where he lay. He was carefully placed on the stretcher in an upright position as he continued to spew bright red blood. By the time he'd been hauled into the emergency vehicle, the front of his blood-splattered, white undershirt was covered and drenched in his blood. When my son and I had seen him ride away, we dressed and drove to the hospital to be with him.

When we arrived, I was certain I knew the diagnosis. The cancer had returned. His once pure-white, now crimson red, undershirt had been pivotal. This time his stay in the hospital was the longest ever. My visit with my husband was daily. One Saturday, our son and I were later than usual getting to the hospital. On this day he felt better, so he called home and asked anxiously, "Hey, when are you coming to see me?" "Soon! Marlon and I are getting dressed now," I assured him. When we were there, he was playful. He incessantly tried to allay my fears, concealing his pain and suffering. He had never wanted to dishearten me, but I had always been an alarmist. However, I was more at ease than in many earlier months. I hadn't made peace with the possible loss of my beloved; neither was I crumbling. Delving into God's Word, developing a deeper and more intimate relationship with Him had made my struggle less difficult. I had come to terms with suffering. I hadn't been the first, nor would I be the last. Greater ones than I had suffered to a greater degree than I.

I recalled how the Apostle Paul had suffered. In 2 Corinthians 11:23-33, he speaks of his imprisonment, countless beatings nearly to death, shipwreck, stoning and being left for dead, many dangers, hunger, thirst, cold exposure, and there was daily pressure on him of his anxiety for all the churches. Yet his suffering had a purpose. He suffered for his Lord's name, the magnification of the resurrection power of his Savior. Paul even says, "We should rejoice in suffering, knowing that suffering produces endurance, endurance produces character, character produces hope, and hope does not put us to shame, shame, because God's love has been poured into our hearts through the Holy Spirit who has been given to us" (Romans 5:1-5).

Suffering for the two of us was not over. I vividly recall a visit with my husband as he continued to lie in a hospital bed. I'm pretty sure that Mark had seen the handwriting on the wall by then. He was keenly aware that his days on this earth were numbered. His pet name for me was "Jack." He turned to me from his hospital bed and said, "Jack, if anything happened to you, I would not marry again." That was my sweetie, always diplomatic. After forty-four and one-half years of marriage, this wonderfully extraordinary man knew that I very well understood how to read between the lines. He had suggested that I should not marry again when he departs.

On another day, while he still lay in bed uncommunicative, I found it necessary to examine him for pressure ulcers as always because he had a preferred position. When his attending physician made rounds, I used my index finger to point out the area of the bedsore that had developed along mid-thigh. He swiftly brushed my hand away and yelled, "Don't touch it!" I had not touched it and felt terribly disappointed. I hadn't wanted my loved one to feel uncomfortable. I instantly led the doctor beyond the door, out of earshot, so that he could discuss anything else he needed to add about my husband's health condition without upsetting my beloved. I was exceedingly agitated because when I was a child, information had been widely spread in my small community that hearing is the last sense that is lost in the dying process.

Some minutes later, a nurse walked into his room, and apparently the doctor gave her instructions. She then noticed the care and love I gave to my husband and asked, "How long have you two been married?" I replied proudly, "Forty-four and a half years, and on June fifteenth we will have been married for forty-five years." "I don't think he's going to make it!" she recklessly retorted. Where was her sensitivity and compassion? It was bad enough that both my husband and I knew his health was rapidly deteriorating. So why did she have to rub salt in the wound? At that moment I turned my face to the wall, tears filled my eyes and sprang forward, streaming down my face. Although I was no longer clambering to escape that impenetrable dark, tortuous bottomless pit of despair, I needed not to be reminded of my beloved's imminent death. Although Satan is personified evil that seeks to control all happenings on earth, he has no power over God's children. God is sovereign over all things, even Satan. "Satan is the ancient serpent, who is the devil and Satan, and deceiver of all the whole world" (Revelation 12:9).

By this time, my darling had spent nearly three months in the hospital and I had visited him daily. At the close of the school day, I gathered my tote bag with pens for grading students' papers and headed for the hospital. Once I was there, I walked over to greet my sweet husband, put down my bag so that I could purchase dinner from the dining room, eat in his room and spend all of my time with Mark while checking and grading papers before departing for the night.

Near the end of Mark's three-month hospitalization, his primary provider approached and advised me to move "Dr. Ivey" to a healthcare center, for it would be better. He was confident that I was incapable of caring for him at home. He tried to persuade me that the attending physician at that facility would be sure Dr. Ivey would receive proper care and would see that he suffered no pain; also, nurses would be there to care for him. I cannot say that he knew, but I became terribly perturbed! He was being transferred to hospice care! He had determined he was terminally ill, and it was a certainty he had given up on my husband. Who was this man? He was not God! As soon as I had come home from my visit at the hospital, I instantaneously telephoned Moffitt Cancer Center of Tampa, Florida, and attempted to have Mark transported and admitted. Why Moffitt? According to my findings, H. Lee Moffitt Center and Research Institute is a cancer facility and teaching hospital that is ranked as one of the best hospitals in Florida for receiving treatment for cancer. The person with whom I talked gleaned all pertinent information, and a transferal was in the works. I cannot decipher what happened after my call. I only know that a transferal of my husband to Moffitt was not to be realized. I had to accept that. I surmised that when hospital admissions and Mark's physician discussed a possible transfer, admittance was denied because his state of health was deemed moribund.

At his physician's insistence and my disinclination, he had been transported and admitted to the healthcare center that the physician had recommended. On his first day and my first visit at the center, my husband was combative. He resisted and fought back to prevent the nurse from clearing his mouth. Heretofore, this had never been his behavior. Not once before had he complained, but I had heard one moan as he was being transported to this facility. It was obvious that my mother-in-law, whom I had contacted hours earlier, sat nearby, was largely disturbed as well as I. I presumed she wished that I should have suggested that the nurse be more gentle while caring for her son. Nonetheless, I had often heard of similar conduct when one is approaching death, it is likely due to decreased flow of blood to the brain, metabolic changes or some other reasons.

The second day of my visit, I inquired of his whereabouts since he had been moved. He then had been assigned a private room and was completely unaware that I was visiting him. On the fourth visit of the fourth day, he slept constantly and there was no response to any stimuli. I left as an empty vessel. My sad eyes were pools of water that readily filled to the brim and overflowed the deck. I could barely drive home through the blurry tears that night.

When I arrived at our home, my face was stained with tears. I knocked at the door until our son opened the door to the laundry room. I was utterly distraught and he asked no questions. I became greatly disconcerted and strongly reprimanded him. "Mom, what do you want me to do? When I ask about Dad, you cry, and when I don't ask, you cry," he mildly retaliated.

Chapter 13
Our Final Hours as Husband and Wife

The following morning, I knew I couldn't teach even one class. It was imperative that I spend the hours that were left with the love of my life. So I called Lakeland Highlands Middle School to report my absence. Just prior to that revered Friday, it was a certainty that wild horses could not have kept me away! I knew that death was imminent because my beloved's sleep had increased, and he could no longer be aroused. I had been compelled to take that personal day away from my place of employment to sit with my darling of a husband on his fifth day as a patient at the healthcare center.

Before I would leave that Friday morning my pastor, who was always affable, had called my home and promised to meet at the center and offered to bring hot soup or a salad. I was most appreciative but graciously declined his kind gesture. I had no appetite.

Some few minutes later that morning, I floundered into the center with some apprehension and faltered into my husband's room despairingly and warily. He was breathing but breaths were slow, short and shallow. His eyes had lost tension and were partly exposed as he slept. There was no pupillary reaction to light. His jaw was relaxed, and his mouth was partly open. His body temperature was cooler to the touch than ever before. It was obvious that time was slowing down, and he was approaching the end of his personal journey in this world. In the midst of my sorrow, I somehow found some comfort to share this time alone with him.

Soon, our pastor hastily walked through the door. He reached for a chair and sat next to me. With Bible in hand, he gently slid his fingers beneath the pages, flipping them, delicately searching until he had located the appropriate Scripture. He read several verses with intensity and power. When he had finished, he slowly looked up and reverently suggested, "Let us pray." With a fully outstretched arm, he took my hand in his and held it firmly. With my free hand, I reached for my husband's hand. With his in mine, I tightly clung to it as he slept peacefully and without interruption. When the pastor had finished a brief but very fervent prayer, I immediately raised my head, opened my eyes and looked toward my husband. I no longer saw the rise and fall of his chest or heard the slow, short, shallow breaths. I instantly stood to place a finger beneath his nose and there was nothing—not even the slightest puff of air. I got no pulse from his wrist or his carotid artery. It appeared that his breaths had ceased and his heart had stopped. My pastor asked with much astonishment, "Is he not breathing?" "No," I replied with disappointment. "Should I get the nurse?" he asked with urgency. "Yes, please," I responded. Within seconds, he hurried back and the two of them burst into the room. The nurse stood closely beside my husband's bed and prepared for chest auscultation. She removed the stethoscope that was draped around her neck, tapped it gently to determine the active side and slid the ear tips into both of her ears so that they fitted snugly. With a sufficient amount of pressure, she placed the silver two-sided chest piece to my husband's chest, listened and slowly ripped them away and lowered her head while turning it from side to side. We all knew then that he was resting in the arms of his Savior and was now at peace for eternity. The nurse then methodically and gingerly began to remove the gastrostomy feeding tube (that had been inserted months earlier through his stomach) and then his socks. She tried to pull his eyelids down to completely close his eyes and futilely attempted to close his mouth that was still agape.

Then, she readily began to pull up the top sheet of his bed to cover his cool, lifeless body. I begged with a brittle voice, "Please, don't cover his face." My eyes had begun to well with tears, flood and gush down my cheeks. I was overcome with grief and sorrow over the loss of my companion, my lover, the father of our three sons and my husband of forty-four and a half years. I threw myself upon his bed and wailed as if my heart would literally break. How could I let go? We had spent more than half our lives as one.

Moments passed. With a tear-stained face, I raised my head, leaned in and tenderly kissed his cool forehead, his eyelids and hand. I forbade anyone to take him away, nor would I leave his side. The nurse at that moment promised me that my precious one would remain in bed and my presence as long as I chose to have him. She left and returned after an hour and leaned forward through the ajar door. I shouted out through my tears, "I'm not ready yet!" "Take your time—

whenever you're ready," she suggested softly and benevolently.

In the meantime, my brother-in-law, my church elder and other elders of Covenant Presbyterian Church were summoned. They were by my side. I thank God that I was not alone, nor was my beloved.

Hours beyond my husband's last breath, I sat at his side. I did not want to leave, for this would be my last opportunity to spend time with him before he would be whisked away. I left it to the healthcare facility to telephone the H. W. Oldham Funeral Home of Lakeland, Florida, for the removal of my beloved's cold, lifeless body.

I wearily returned to my home, accompanied by my brother-in-law, who followed in his vehicle. We sat and reminisced as tears of sorrow continued to spring forward and spill down an already stained face. I was distraught and mournful and did not feel prepared to accept my new identity as "widow," for I had deduced that I had lost the love of my life far too soon. Much time had elapsed before I'd come to realize that I had the charge to make funeral arrangements for my husband.

Chapter 14
My Husband's Funeral - The Long Goodbye

My mother-in-law had wanted a funeral for family and friends in their hometown, the rural community of Santos, Florida. I knew that I could not fail to allow friends and former patients to celebrate our loved one with the traditions associated with laying my husband to rest. After all, Lakeland, Florida, is where Dr. Mark Ivey III had practiced medicine for the past twenty-one years. Appropriately, there had to be two separate occasions to celebrate the life of my husband.

A viewing on the following Wednesday evening preceded the services that took place at the church the next day at Covenant Presbyterian Church. Many attended the simple and beautiful ceremony. The bronze casket that had been selected by our sons, Marlon and Michael, had been placed at the front of the church. The immediate Ivey family provided a large spray of fresh red roses with baby's breath, which sat on top of the casket. Many friends expressed their love, support and condolences with potted plants, colorful flower baskets and containers of fresh, seasonal flowers. These, which flanked both sides of the casket, afforded great comfort and enlivened the mood of the occasion.

At three o'clock in the afternoon on January 16, 2003, friends and mourners who had assembled in Covenant Presbyterian Church rose as the family of Dr. Mark Ivey III processioned into the sanctuary. Prior to the ceremony, the funeral director asked me if I'd like to see my husband once again before the final closing of the casket. "Yes," I replied. I calmly stood, walked over to the casket and looked at him adoringly before leaning forward to kiss him on the lips once more. Soon the short, sweet ceremony began. Old and New Testament scriptures were read from the Holy Bible. The music was consistent of a solo of Malotte's *The Lord's Prayer* and beautiful hymns. Some alumni, associates and friends shared memories of those things they loved most about our loved one that honored him, and the pastor delivered the eulogy.

Afterwards, the Women in the Church (WIC) graciously readied and served a delectable sympathy meal in the church's fellowship hall to a gathering of loved ones and close friends of our deceased Mark.

Immediately after the funeral services, one of Ocala's local funeral directors had arrived to transport my deceased husband to Ocala. He would be held there until and for the second service. This was a collaborative effort between the two funeral directors.

On the Saturday that followed of the same week, additional family, friends and grievers gathered for the second ceremony at Calvary Missionary Baptist Church in Santos, Florida. The program was practically a template of the first, and again there was time for conversation and sharing of thoughts and stories about and expressions of condolences for the loss of our deceased loved one while gathered for that informal mercy meal.

When the repast was over, those of us who had driven or ridden to Santos climbed into our vehicles for the trip back to Lakeland. Funeral Director H. W. Oldham led the way through the back roads of Florida. A local funeral director of Ocala who was hired to help create a meaningful funeral experience followed in the coach that transported the casket of the remains of my husband to the place of burial.

It was somewhat late in the afternoon when we reached the burial ground, and only two of our sons were present. We took seats beneath the tent. For the duration of both observances, I had evinced great courage and fortitude, but when as I observed the coffin as it rested above the grave on the casket-lowering device and waited for my lover and the father of our three sons to be interred, I quietly began to shed tears. The funeral director's assistant draped her arm over my shoulder and said, "You've done so well," as she led me away from the grave. I never was afforded the opportunity to see his coffin as it was lowered into the deep, cold hard earth. That ritual of burial is so permanent and depressing.

Nonetheless, I had grown because of the suffering and great depression. I learned that suffering is profitable. Does that sound insane? It isn't! Paul exhorts us to rejoice in suffering.

There is outgrowth as a result of suffering. Believers know that God is our Father and when we are troubled we go to Him in prayer because He says, "Cast your cares upon Me, for I care for you." When we go to God in prayer, His response is in His own time, not ours. If this is a long process, we learn to endure. When we hold on, this gives rise to one's character or traits. Our character or traits produce hope, and hope does not put us to shame because the love of God had been poured into our hearts through the Holy Spirit, who has been given to us (Romans 5:3-5). Therefore, those of us who have hope in the glory of God can rejoice now. Matthew Henry said, "A right sense of God's love to us, will make us not ashamed, either of our hope, or of our sufferings for Him" (*Christianity.com*).

Throughout the service, I was in a state of tranquility, the peace of God, for I had meditated on God's Word consistently, and His Word is true. "The peace of God, which passes all understanding, shall keep your hearts and minds through Christ Jesus" (Philippians 4:7).

Of course, I was grieved but not as those who have no hope. I continue to have great sorrow for the loss of my beloved, even now. I miss his smile, laughter, quirks, humor, love, kisses, embraces, our togetherness, and the list goes on and on. However, I know that my grief will end some day in the future. The Apostle Paul said, "For since we believe that Jesus died and rose again, even so, through Jesus, God will bring with him those who have fallen asleep" (1 Thessalonians 4:14). I've often heard it said that people who fall asleep wake up. In reference to those who have fallen asleep, John Calvin said, "Is not to the soul but to the body, for the dead rests in the tomb as on a bed until God raises the person up." Believers can find hope in the return of Jesus Christ and the resurrection of those who have fallen asleep, the dead. If one does not believe biblical history, this is denial of God's existence, but if God created the heavens, the earth, the sea and all therein, He is sovereign over all things. If this is true, He most unquestionably has the power to resurrect the dead, removing the sting of death and gaining victory over the grave (1 Corinthians 15:55). Paul says that the dead in Christ will rise first. Then we who are alive, who are left, will be caught up together with them in the clouds to meet the Lord in the air, and so we will always be with the Lord (I Thessalonians 4:16). This is the greatest news of all, to know that we will live with the Lord and our loved ones again for all eternity unless a loved one died without Christ. It is unfortunate that unbelievers have no such hope.

I would say that the truth is not in me if I said that I got over my beloved's death. Even twenty years later, I experience moments of loneliness and yearn to have him near. I've even wished that I could see his figure filling the doorway of our bedroom just once more. Sometimes tears well up and trickle down my face when I hear specific music that we most enjoyed. While lying in bed, I reach over on the other side to find complete emptiness. Often I visit his grave alone, while expressing my love and despair for his absence. I will never get over this loss, but I have learned to cope through the Scriptures that are written upon my heart. Writing for me is cathartic, and it permits me to translate my loss and heartbreak into expressions of love.

Chapter 15
My Poems to Commemorate My Husband, the Love of My Life

The Thirteenth Anniversary of My Beloved's Death

I wondered how I'd continue this life's journey when you went away;
I prayed for compassion and mercies with the dawn of every new day

You could not have known that I love you and pine for you still;
The mere thought of you sends a rapturous, spine-tingling thrill

"I love you" is a powerful, bewitching melody that replays in my head;
I won't accept the thought that a life of joy and blissfulness is dead

With each passing day, my heavy, aching heart is filled with misery;
I cannot stop thinking of you, and that's the unadulterated reality

Oh, Lord, holy and true, I am still ill-prepared to face my own fears;
How much longer must I drown in my own bucket of tears?

Thirteen years later, my poor, sad heart bleeds and is writhed with grief,
And although the years are fleeting, time bestows little relief

By some miracle, Lord, again I'd like to feel the warmth of his embrace;
Without my husband and life partner, my home is an empty, lonely place

Almighty God, I know it is You in Whom I must place my hope and trust;
I'm learning to depend on You until my body, too, returns to dust

I Can't Stop Loving You!

I will forevermore carry an eternal torch of sentimental love for you,
Reinvigorating, refreshing and nourishing like nature's morning dew

For the red flaming arrows of love from your heart evermore pierced mine;
That's when our two adoring hearts started to securely intertwine

From that time onward, our companionate hearts would beat gloriously as one,
And I knew that our extreme relationship of intimacy would be an epic run

I can't verbalize how much I miss being wrapped in your warm embrace;
Thoughts of your soft, tender kisses tingle my spine and cause my heart to race

You set the bar high that there's no chance another man could ever reach,
And so, it is with certainty that my vow to remain a widow I shan't ever breach

Only our loving and compassionate Father could know how much I adore you
Because only a sovereign God can see from a distance my point of view.

Thank God, It Was Just a Dream

Each night I fervidly pray and then gently turn the bed covers back;
This is the customary routine each time before I briskly hit the sack

I fluff the pillows and then close my eyes, hoping you'll soon appear;
It's the now silenced, distinctive, resonant voice that I again long to hear

I look retrospectively and warmly upon memories we once did share;
I recall running my fingers delicately through your silver, wavy hair

I'm locked snugly in your arms and I whisper sweetly into your ear;
Wrapped in your love, I beam with pride just having you ever so near

These are impassioned moments I wish wholeheartedly would never end;
I'm sure no one will wrench away our interwoven hearts or even them rend

When you touch me, fireworks ignite and display bright colorful sparks,
And they're as beautiful as the melodious song of an exaltation of skylarks,

And I vaunt of the sparks that instantly fly, and in your arms is where I belong;
With a sensual love between you and me, nothing could go wrong

Your tender lips press gently against mine as you cradle me in your arms;
I knew when I first saw your handsome face, I'd fall victim of your charms

But alas, sleep overtakes me, and images become part of a dreadful dream;
My subliminal thoughts grow ominous and evil and much too extreme

The pursuit of another lifetime dream again is reason for you to go away;
I'm woebegone since I've not heard you utter a word even to this day

Here I stand abandoned and forlorn, so I have become bitter and blue;
Surely, you can't imagine the somber moroseness you're putting me through

Hours turn into days, days turn into weeks and from you, nary a peep;
I'm trying to navigate through the sorrow that has reached knee-deep

My eyes are pools of water that flood and tears stream down my face;
My greatest fear is that some wretched, wicked woman is taking my place

Every pore of my being oozes rejection and disappointment;
If this is a threat to the sanctity of our marriage, I'll not be content!

When this daunting and repulsive nightmare had rattled me awake,
Thank you, LORD, it was only a terrifying, vivid dream for heaven's sake

What absurdity, my ghastly imaginings shouldn't have been outlandishly grim,
For God had snatched you from a depraved world and you now abide with Him.

Till I Too Shall Take My Rest

The sun isn't a gaseous sphere of enormous heat that irradiates God's earth
If I didn't give my heart to the only man on this planet who knew its worth,

The moon isn't an astronomical orb that is a reflection of a flaming, golden sun
If I don't constantly pine for you, my husband, who was second to none,

A colony of mockingbirds cannot interrupt silence with a soulful melody
That I don't hang my head consistently and lament, "Poor, little, old me,"

Raindrops aren't clinging water molecules that fall from dark, overcast skies
If I don't become lachrymose and tears course and gently drop from my eyes,

And a dark, velvety red rose never releases a sweet pervading perfume
That I don't think of you while wading in the depths of my solemn gloom,

My Father did not preordain this precise moment that we would be apart
If your permanent leave of absence has not taken a slice of my heart,

Seasons aren't yearly cycles that usher in significant changes in the weather
If I don't think that our bodies and souls will one day again come together,

And no matter how often I'm reminded how time heals and how it flies,
I'll continue to commiserate, my love, over your most malapropos demise

As surely as my Lord shows His sustaining grace and daily opens my eyes,
The pain I feel for you, my husband's return, I will never be able to disguise,

And just as long as the stars of the heavens brightly sparkle and glitter,
I'll always be thankful for our precious memories as one and won't be bitter

Albeit we both rejoiced at our wedding and vowed, “Till death us do part,”
Loss and bereavement have become enemies to my wounded heart

Though the origin of my somberness was a fateful event, my heart remains true
When I think of the taste of your soft lips and your embrace, I’m infinitely blue,

Because my Lord is gracious, love, omniscient and He knows what is best,
He’ll comfort me with His steadfast love till I, too, shall take my eternal rest

Happy Heavenly Eighty-fifth Birthday, My Love!

God made the gilt-edged heavens, the earth, the sea and all that is in them;
His glorious purpose and master plan was an absolutely perfect system

He flung a brilliant moon, stars and sun against a black sky to swallow the dark;
He made the animals of every kind that came in tandem and entered Noah's ark

He made primeval trees and sweet scented flowers that are kissed by the sun;
He made green hills and tall impassable mountains, and yet He was not done

He created man and then woman to have dominion over earthly things,
And no one has ever witnessed the immensity of God's infinite offerings

Beyond number were the things an omnipotent, self-existent Father did create;
There was never evolution, a need to defend it or even an attempt to debate!

How I now rejoice that on April 15, 1935, the living God gave you the gift of life;
Honey, it must have been so that I would one day become your loving wife.

And inevitably, the purest praise will be upon my lips forever and forever—
I will cease to honor, earnestly pray and thank a most gracious God never!

Happy Heavenly Birthday, My Beloved!

It was inconceivable that your personal, earthly journey would soon end
However, I was keenly aware that my bleeding heart would never mend

The portentous morning when I warily plodded through your bedroom door,
I knew that our past memories mustn't be sullied since we'd make no more

You lay there uncommunicative and your breathing was utterly shallow,
Your eyes were partly open, and for us two there would be no tomorrow

Nearby, while clasping a Holy Bible, our pastor looked on in silence and sat,
His fingers leafed through the pages and found the perfect words, just like that

When he'd reverently read them, closing the Book, he exhorted, "Let us pray!"
When I opened my eyes, I fixed them upon my beloved and didn't look away

It struck me hard that there wasn't breathing of any kind to speak of anymore
For almost one half-century, he'd been the only man that I would ever adore

Rising from my chair, I searched pitifully for a pulse or any semblance of life
"Oh, no," I cried, he couldn't have abandoned his sons' mother and his wife!

Pastor hastily left the room to summon the nurse and now both had returned,
I didn't want to hear what I'd logically deduced and might've already learned

She checked my husband's auscultations and ripped her stethoscope away,
Her findings would be the cold, hard truth as she shook her head in dismay

My eyes were cisterns that sprang forth bitter tears that ran down my face,
This, by no means, was a time like others we'd treasured and embrace

Leaning forward, I pressed my lips against his cool, dead lips and his forehead,
For forty-four and one-half years this family of five, my beloved had wisely led

She removed his gastronomy feeding tube and began to cover his lifeless body
I begged, "Don't cover his face," for there was already duly dignity and privacy!

"Please don't take him away," I pleaded, as I remained immovably by his side,
"I'm not ready to let go yet," I shouted, as I continually boohooed and cried!

Hours after that visit, the nurse returned and my hubby's body was stone-cold,
And those last hours that I spent with him are memories I shall forever behold!

My True Love

My beloved, I must tell you that I visited your gravesite the other day,
The wind howled eerily and a dreary sky was striated with hues of gray

I gazed fixedly upon the cold, damp ground where your decaying body lay
And rifled through my mind to find alacrity, for it'd been your untimely demise

I'd been smitten to my heart's core by your love since our days of greenness;
Then, my knees buckled as I began to drown in a sea of woeful loneliness

When I lifted my tear-stained face and saw the tombstone that stood above,
Two carved intertwining hearts now symbolized our once self-sacrificial love

With our inscribed names and your birth and death dates upon this marker
Are proof that we'd be together again even after this earth's departure

I clearly wanted those left behind to know that God created you for me,
And two souls will be restored and in the presence of God for all eternity

Then, swiftly I was met with a tsunami of memories that flooded my mind,
During that transient moment, bursts of joy and inner peace I did find

I'd recalled I'd come to remind you that your heavenly birthday was near,
And our two doting, inseparable souls would commemorate another year

My Heart Still Yearns for You

Two thousand and twenty is most emphatically the year,
For it's been seventeen years when I stare at the space in the rear

I never once imagined that I'd survive a day without you,
And often times I still feel beaten, blackened and blue

I long to feel your soft lips and get lost in your warm embrace—
That my sanity hasn't been wrested from my mind is all of God's amazing grace

I yet miss your adoring smile that was never meant for no one except me,
My woeful heart grieves, knowing that this earthly moment again shall never be

I miss my bravely sailing through the air with you, my love, to distant lands,
Sightseeing and enjoying God's masterful handiwork while holding hands

I miss the years of the Lord's Days where at our home church we'd worship,
And each first Sunday we partake of the bread and the wine we'd sip

I miss your coming home from the office and my greeting you at the door
I privately mourn that those times in space will never be anymore

I delicately ask why there was need for you to precipitately leave my side;
I have never comprehended why you sickened and quietly died

Nonetheless, my hope is in Him, my LORD and Savior, who is yet to come,
For He, too, with gladness will receive me when my work here is done

Father, I am so thankful that he's now in your presence and loving care,
For on the day of my expiration, I'll again see my sweetie when I get there!

Nevermore

No more will I feel your embrace as we stare mutually into each other's eyes,
And it is this sickening, tortuous sensation that I can no longer disguise

Nevermore will I feel your warm, soft lips press passionately against mine—
Those expressions of love from the heart were alluring and ever so divine

No longer can I conceal the stabbing pain that pierces my aching heart
Since my Father called you home and two loving souls were torn apart

No more will I hear sweet utterances that you whispered softly in my ear—
Those words that were titillating, steamy, naughty and always so sincere

Nevermore will we lovebirds dine in a room that's illuminated by candlelight
Nevertheless, there is a forever burning flame in my heart that you did ignite

Never again can two doting lovers stroll hand-in-hand through the park
Nor gaze at a dying, crimson sunset that's being swallowed up by the dark

Nevermore will we lovers snuggle nor cuddle before falling asleep in bed,
Nor will I spoon with my husband and upon his strong chest lay my head

I'll never again smell the rich scent of the beautiful roses you'd give to me,
Nor hear words like a honeycomb that created a massive, romantic symphony

I'll never again breathe in a smile that was meant for me and so endearing
And never, never again "I love you, my darling" are words I will be hearing

My state of mind is still sentimental and an emotional place of flaming torment,
I'll never erase the memories of precious moments together two lovers spent

You showed appreciation, honesty, love, loyalty, patience, respect and pride,
You were slow to anger, for often it was folly to you, so you'd cast it aside

You had learned gentle words deflect wrath, but harsh words could be costly,
So you maintained self-control, speaking to me compassionately and often softly

Our bloom of youth was filled with deep affection and absolute enjoyment,
But not since my Lord reclaimed the irreplaceable gift that was heavenly sent

My husband, I will never lose hope, for the brightest of days await me, too;
That's the day when I'm called home and I'll meet up with my Lord and you

Conclusion

Although my greatest fear had been losing the love of my life, God blessed me and allayed my fears when I first began to diligently seek Him and His righteousness. I knew the Lord, but had become negligent when I set my thoughts possibly more upon my spouse, his health issues, constant thoughts of his possible imminent death, imaginings that I was incapable of survival without him, and I apparently did not trust my Father wholeheartedly, for He knows all things.

How could I have been mistrustful of my Father, "For He formed my inward parts and knitted me together in my mother's womb fearfully and wonderfully" (Psalm 139:13)? Unlike Faith, which is a gift of God, trust is an act or a process as a result of faith.

In retrospect, this meant I needed to increase my confidence and learn to rely solely on Him. Even though I had read the Bible three times from the Old and through the New Testaments, I likely saw God's Word as a Book of history and a written account of wonderful stories, which they are, but there was and is a great need to know the Bible and apply God's Word to my life. Of course, I had read the Bible, but I needed to get to know God, His ways and His purpose for me. This meant that I must act upon His Word. 2 Timothy 3:16

says, "All Scripture is breathed out by God and profitable for teaching, for reproof, for correction, and for training in righteousness." For me then and now, this means to read, interpret, learn or memorize Scripture and apply it.

So, my late husband and I regularly attended Bible studies at a former church whose pastor was the Reverend G. L. Champion, one who was well-versed in Scripture and Head of the Eleventh Episcopal District of Christian Education in Florida. My husband and I would later move our membership to Covenant Presbyterian Church here in Lakeland, Florida, where we continued to attend worship services with regularity, worshiping God with other believers and being taught God's inerrant Word every Lord's Day for our spiritual growth.

Subsequent to my retirement from Polk County Public Schools, I began to frequent the Women's Bible Studies at Covenant. Here, numerous Bible study tools and retreats were made available to further deepen one's relationship with God. Recognition of the mood verbs: indicatives and imperatives greatly helped me in these studies when I learned that an indicative always precedes the imperative, which is a simple statement of fact. It is what God is doing, has already done or is going to do on my and your behalf in Christ. It is a verb of certainty, while the imperative mood is a statement of what we must do. There is a definite relationship between those two moods in the area of sanctification. By this pattern of consistency, God denotes that sanctification depends on God, but we must cooperate by doing our part. Also, learning that there is voluminous power in God's promises was huge! So, I began to incorporate God's promises into my prayers since I had read that He is moved when we do so.

In summary, I try diligently and continually to implement all of the above because Paul says in Philippians 4:9, "Whatever you have learned or received or heard from me, or seen in me—put it into practice. And the God of peace will be with you."

Now, I am finally at peace. This does not suggest that I am completely numb to the loss of my husband because there are periods in my life when I would love to return to the past. However, at this moment in time, when among friends, I can burst into unrestrained laughter, being the loudest among those in the group, when having pure innocent enjoyment! All praise and thanks to God!

About the Author

Jacqueline Ivey is a retired teacher and author of *Book of Original Poems and Memoirs*. She taught at the Campbell Senior High and Turie T. Small Elementary Schools in Daytona Beach, Florida; Gra-Mar and Haynes Elementary Schools in Nashville, Tennessee; Firestone, Barber, Fraunfelter and Henry Elementary Schools in Akron Ohio, and she finished her teaching career after a twenty-three-year stint at the Lakeland Highlands Middle School in Lakeland, Florida.

Jacqueline's colorful *The Great Depression* draws from her own personal experience of clinical depression while caring for her loving husband, whose physical health is steadily deteriorating. She cannot accept the reality that he might die an early death.

Jacqueline is a widow, mother, former teacher and an author. She attended Florida Agriculture and Mechanical University and graduated from Bethune-Cookman College, the now Bethune-Cookman University. She also took a writing course at Warner University, Lake Wales, Florida.

She, too, has traveled extensively, visiting many parts of North America, South America, the Far East of East Asia, Northeastern Africa and Western Europe.